A SHORT HISTORY

OF

GREEK PHILOSOPHY

BY
JOHN MARSHALL

M.A. OXON., LL.D. EDIN.
RECTOR OF THE ROYAL HIGH SCHOOL, EDINBURGH
FORMERLY PROFESSOR OF CLASSICAL LITERATURE
AND PHILOSOPHY
IN THE YORKSHIRE COLLEGE, LEEDS

LONDON
PERCIVAL AND CO.
1891

This book has been published by:

Greenbook Publications,llc

ISBN# 1-61743-056-0

ISBN# 978-1-61743-056-5

This edition Copyright © 2012

Printed in the United States of America.

At Greenbook Publications it is our goal to find original hard to read books and republish them in an easy to read format. We believe in the importance of supporting the environment therefore 3% of all proceeds are donated to helping the environment!

Any questions or commits can be emailed to Greenbookpublications@mail.com

Or you can visit our web site at Greenbookpublications.com

Contents

PREFACE

The main purpose which I have had in view in writing this book has been to present an account of Greek philosophy which, within strict limits of brevity, shall be at once authentic and interesting—*authentic*, as being based on the original works themselves, and not on any secondary sources; *interesting*, as presenting to the ordinary English reader, in language freed as far as possible from technicality and abstruseness, the great thoughts of the greatest men of antiquity on questions of permanent significance and value. There has been no attempt to shirk the really philosophic problems which these men tried in their day to solve; but I have endeavored to show, by a sympathetic treatment of them, that these problems were no mere wars of words, but that in fact the philosophers of twenty-four centuries ago were dealing with exactly similar difficulties as to the bases of belief and of right action as, under different forms, beset thoughtful men and women to-day.

In the general treatment of the subject, I have followed in the main the order, and drawn chiefly on the selection of passages, in Ritter and Preller's *Historia Philosophiae Graecae*. It is hoped that in this way the little book may be found useful at the universities, as a running commentary on that excellent work; and the better to aid students in the use of it for that purpose, the corresponding sections in Ritter and Preller are indicated by the figures in the margin.

In the sections on Plato, and occasionally elsewhere, I have drawn to some extent, by the kind permission of the Delegates of the Clarendon Press and his own, on Professor Jowett's great commentary and translation.

JOHN MARSHALL.

8

CHAPTER I

THE SCHOOL OF MILETUS

The question of Thales—Water the beginning of things—Soul in all things—Mystery in science—Abstraction and reality—Theory of development

I. THALES.—For several centuries prior to the great Persian invasions of Greece, perhaps the very greatest and wealthiest city of the Greek world was Miletus. Situate about the centre of the Ionian coasts of Asia Minor, with four magnificent harbors and a strongly defensible position, it gathered to itself much of the great overland trade, which has flowed for thousands of years eastward and westward between India and the Mediterranean; while by its great fleets it created a new world of its own along the Black Sea coast. Its colonies there were so numerous that Miletus was named 'Mother of Eighty Cities.' From Abydus on the Bosphorus, past Sinope, and so onward to the Crimea and the Don, and thence round to Thrace, a busy community of colonies, mining, manufacturing, ship-building, corn-raising, owned Miletus for their mother-city. Its marts must therefore have been crowded with merchants of every country from India to Spain, from Arabia to Russia; the riches and the wonders of every clime must have become familiar to its inhabitants. And fitly enough, therefore, in this city was born the first notable Greek geographer, the first constructor of a map, the first observer of natural and other curiosities, the first recorder of varieties of custom among various communities, the first speculator on the causes of strange phenomena,—Hecataeus. His work is in great part lost, but we know a good deal about it from the frequent references to him and it in the work of his rival and follower, Herodotus.

The city naturally held a leading place politically as well as commercially. Empire in our sense was alien to the instincts of the Greek race; but Miletus was for centuries recognized as the foremost member of a great commercial and political league, the political character of the league becoming more defined, as first the Lydian and then the Persian monarchy became an aggressive neighbor on its borders.

It was in this active, prosperous, enterprising state, and at the period of its highest activity, that Thales, statesman, practical engineer, mathematician, philosopher, flourished. Without attempting to fix his date too closely, we may take it that he was a leading man in Miletus for the greater part of the first half of the sixth century before Christ. We hear of an eclipse predicted by him, of the course of a river usefully changed, of shrewd and profitable handling of the market, of wise advice in the general councils of the league. He seems to have been at once a student of mathematics and an observer of nature, and withal something having analogy with both, an inquirer or speculator into the *origin* of things. To us nowadays this suggests a student of geology, or physiography, or some such branch of physical science; to Thales it probably rather suggested a theoretical inquiry into the simplest *thinkable* aspect of things as existing. "Under what form known to us," he would seem to have asked, "may we assume an identity in all known things, so as best to cover or render explicable the things as we know them?" The 'beginning' of things (for it was thus he described this assumed identity) was not conceived by him as something which was long ages before, and which had ceased to be; rather it meant the reality of things now. Thales then was the putter of a question, which had not been asked expressly before, but which has never ceased to be asked since. He was also the formulator of a new meaning for a word; the word 'beginning' ((Greek) *arche*) got the meaning of 'underlying reality' and so of 'ending' as well. In short, he so dealt with a word, on the surface of it implying time, as to eliminate the idea of time, and suggest a method of looking at the world, more profound and far-reaching than had been before imagined.[1]

It is interesting to find that the man who was thus the first philosopher, the first observer who took a metaphysical, non-temporal, analytical view of the world, and so became the predecessor of all those votaries of 'other-world' ways of thinking,—whether as academic idealist, or 'budge doctor of the Stoic fur,' or Christian ascetic or what not, whose ways are such a puzzle to the 'hard-headed practical man,'—was himself one of the shrewdest men of his day, so shrewd that by common consent he was placed foremost in antiquity among the Seven Sages, or seven shrewd men, whose practical wisdom became a world's tradition, enshrined in anecdote and crystallized in proverb.

The chief record that we possess of the philosophic teaching of Thales is contained in an interesting notice of earlier philosophies by Aristotle, the main part of which as regards Thales runs as follows:

"The early philosophers as a rule formulated the originative principle ((Greek) *arche*) of all things under some material expression. By the originative principle or element of things they meant that of which all existing things are composed, that which determines their coming into being, and into which they pass on ceasing to be. Where these philosophers differed from each other was simply in the answer which they gave to the question what was the nature of this principle, the differences of view among them applying both to the number, and to the character, of the supposed element or elements.

"Thales, the pioneer of this philosophy, maintained that *Water* was the originative principle of all things. It was doubtless in this sense that he said that

---

[1] By some authorities it is stated that Anaximander, the second philosopher of this school, was the first to use the word *arche* in the philosophic sense. Whether this be so or not, Thales certainly had the idea.

the earth rested on water. What suggested the conception to him may have been such facts of observation, as that all forms of substance which promote life are moist, that heat itself seems to be conditioned by moisture, that the life-producing seed in all creatures is moist, and so on."

Other characteristics of water, it is elsewhere suggested, may have been in Thales' mind, such as its readiness to take various shapes, its convertibility from water into vapor or ice, its ready mixture with other substances, and so forth. What we have chiefly to note is, that the more unscientific this theory about the universe may strike us as being, the more completely out of accord with facts now familiar to everybody, the more striking is it as marking a new mood of mind, in which *unity*, though only very partially suggested or discoverable by the senses, is preferred to that infinite and indefinite *variety* and *difference* which the senses give us at every moment. There is here the germ of a new aspiration, of a determination not to rest in the merely momentary and different, but at least to try, even against the apparent evidence of the senses, for something more permanently intelligible. As a first suggestion of what this permanent underlying reality may be, *Water* might very well pass. It is probable that even to Thales himself it was only a symbol, like the figure in a mathematical proposition, representing by the first passable physical phenomenon which came to hand, that ideal reality underlying all change, which is at once the beginning, the middle, and the end of all. That he did not mean Water, in the ordinary prosaic sense, to be identical with this, is suggested by some other sayings of his. "Thales," says Aristotle elsewhere, "thought the whole universe was full of gods." "All things," he is recorded as saying, "have a *soul* in them, in virtue of which they move other things, and are themselves moved, even as the magnet, by virtue of its life or soul, moves the iron." Without pushing these fragmentary utterances too far, we may well conclude that whether Thales spoke of the soul of the universe and its divine indwelling powers, or gods, or of water as the origin of things, he was only vaguely symbolizing in different ways an idea as yet formless and void, like the primeval chaos, but nevertheless, like it, containing within it a promise and a potency of greater life hereafter.

II. ANAXIMANDER.—Our information with respect to thinkers so remote as these men is too scanty and too fragmentary, to enable us to say in what manner or degree they influenced each other. We cannot say for certain that any one of them was pupil or antagonist of another. They appear each of them, one might say for a moment only, from amidst the darkness of antiquity; a few sayings of theirs we catch vaguely across the void, and then they disappear. There is not, consequently, any very distinct progression or continuity observable among them, and so far therefore one has to confess that the title 'School of Miletus' is a misnomer. We have already quoted the words of Aristotle in which he classes the Ionic philosophers together, as all of them giving a *material* aspect of some kind to the originative principle of the universe. But while this is a characteristic observable in some of them, it is not so obviously discoverable in the second of their number, Anaximander.

This philosopher is said to have been younger by one generation than Thales, but to have been intimate with him. He, like Thales, was a native of Miletus, and while we do not hear of him as a person, like Thales, of political eminence and activity, he was certainly the equal, if not the superior, of Thales in mathematical and scientific ability. He is said to have either invented or at least made known to Greece the construction of the sun-dial. He was associated with Hecataeus in the construction of the earliest geographical charts or maps; he devoted himself with some success to the science of astronomy. His familiarity with the abstractions of mathematics perhaps accounts for the more abstract form, in which he expressed his idea of the principle of all things.

To Anaximander this principle was, as he expressed it, the *infinite*; not water nor any other of the so-called elements, but a different thing from any of them, something hardly namable, out of whose formlessness the heavens and all the worlds in them came to be. And by necessity into that same infinite or indefinite existence, out of which they originally emerged, did every created thing return. Thus, as he poetically expressed it, "Time brought its revenges, and for the wrong-doing of existence all things paid the penalty of death."

The momentary resting-place of Thales on the confines of the familiar world of things, in his formulation of Water as the principle of existence, is thus immediately removed. We get, as it were, to the earliest conception of things as we find it in Genesis; before the heavens were, or earth, or the waters under the earth, or light, or sun, or moon, or grass, or the beast of the field, when the "earth was without form, and void, and darkness was upon the face of the deep." Only, be it observed, that while in the primitive Biblical idea this formless void precedes in *time* an ordered universe, in Anaximander's conception this formless infinitude is always here, is in fact the only reality whichever is here, something without beginning or ending, underlying all, enwrapping all, governing all.

To modern criticism this may seem to be little better than verbiage, having, perhaps, some possibilities of poetic treatment, but certainly very unsatisfactory if regarded as science. But to this we have to reply that one is not called upon to regard it as science. Behind science, as much to-day when our knowledge of the details of phenomena is so enormously increased, as in the times when science had hardly begun, there lies a world of mystery which we cannot pierce, and yet which we are compelled to assume. No scientific treatise can begin without assuming Matter and Force as data, and however much we may have learned about the relations of *forces* and the affinities of *things*, Matter and Force as such remain very much the same dim infinities, that the originative 'Infinite' was to Anaximander.

It is to be noted, however, that while modern science assumes necessarily *two* correlative data or originative principles,—Force, namely, as well as Matter,— Anaximander seems to have been content with the formulation of but one; and perhaps it is just here that a kinship still remains between him and Thales and other philosophers of the school. He, no more than they, seems to have definitely raised the question, How are we to account for, or formulate, the principle of *difference* or change? What is it that causes things to come into being out of, or recalls them back from being into, the infinite void? It is to be confessed, however, that our accounts on this point are somewhat conflicting. One authority actually says that he formulated motion as eternal also. So far as he attempted to grasp the idea of difference in relation to that of unity, he seems to have regarded the principle of change or difference as inhering in the infinite itself. Aristotle in this connection contrasts his doctrine with that of Anaxagoras, who formulated *two* principles of existence—Matter and Mind. Anaximander, he points out, found all he wanted in the one.

As a mathematician Anaximander must have been familiar in various aspects with the functions of the Infinite or Indefinable in the organization of thought. To the student of Euclid, for example, the impossibility of adequately defining any of the fundamental elements of the science of geometry—the point, the line, the surface—is a familiar fact. In so far as a science of geometry is possible at all, the exactness, which is its essential characteristic, is only attainable by starting from data which are in themselves impossible, as of a point which has no magnitude, of a line which has no breadth, of a surface which has no thickness. So in the science of abstract number the fundamental assumptions, as that $1=1$, $x=x$, etc., are contradicted by every fact of experience, for in the world as we know it, absolute equality is simply impossible to discover; and yet these fundamental conceptions are in their development most powerful instruments for the extension of man's command over his own experiences. Their completeness of abstraction from the accidents of experience, from the differences, qualifications, variations which contribute so largely to the personal interests of life, this it is which makes the abstract sciences demonstrative, exact, and universally applicable. In so far, therefore, as we are permitted to grasp the conception of a perfectly abstract existence prior to, and underlying, and enclosing, all separate existences, so far also do we get to a conception which is demonstrative, exact, and universally applicable throughout the whole world of knowable objects.

Such a conception, however, by its absolute emptiness of content, does not afford any means in itself of progression; somehow and somewhere a principle of movement, of development, of concrete reality, must be found or assumed, to link this ultimate abstraction of existence to the multifarious phenomena of existence as known. And it was, perhaps, because Anaximander failed to work out this aspect of the question, that in the subsequent leaders of the school *movement*, rather than mere existence, was the principle chiefly insisted upon.

Before passing, however, to these successors of Anaximander, some opinions of his which we have not perhaps the means of satisfactorily correlating with his general conception, but which are not without their individual interest, may here be noted. The word *husk* or *bark* ((Greek) *phloios*) seems to have been a favorite one with him, as implying and depicting a conception of interior and necessary development in things. Thus he seems to have postulated an inherent tendency or law in the infinite, which compelled it to develop contrary characters, as hot and cold, dry and moist. In consequence of this fundamental tendency an envelope of fire, he says, came into being, encircling another envelope of air, which latter in turn enveloped the sphere of earth, each being like the 'husk' of the other, or like the bark which encloses the tree. This concentric system he conceives as having in some way been parted up into various systems, represented by the sun, the moon, the stars, and the earth. The last he figured as hanging in space, and deriving its stability from the inherent and perfect balance or relation of its parts.

Then, again, as to the origin of man, he seems to have in like manner taught a theory of development from lower forms of life. In his view the first living creatures must have come into being in moisture (thus recalling the theory of Thales). As time went on, and these forms of life reached their fuller possibilities, they came to be transferred to the dry land, casting off their old nature like a husk or bark. More particularly he insists that man must have developed out of other and lower forms of life, because of his exceptional need, under present conditions, of care and nursing in his earlier years. Had he come into being at once as a human creature he could never have survived.

The analogies of these theories with modern speculations are obvious and interesting. But without enlarging on these, one has only to say in conclusion that, suggestive and interesting as many of these poor fragments, these *disjecti membra poetae*, are individually, they leave us more and more impressed with a sense of incompleteness in our knowledge of Anaximander's theory as a whole. It may be that as a consistent and perfected system the theory never was worked out; it may be that it never was properly understood.

CHAPTER II

THE SCHOOL OF MILETUS (*concluded*)

Air the beginning of things—All things pass—The eternal and the temporary—The weeping philosopher

III. ANAXIMENES.—This philosopher was also a native of Miletus, and is said to have been a hearer or pupil of Anaximander. As we have said, the tendency of the later members of the school was towards emphasizing the *motive* side of the supposed underlying principle of nature, and accordingly Anaximenes chose Air as the element which best represented or symbolized that principle. Its fluidity, readiness of movement, wide extension, and absolute neutrality of character as regards color, taste, smell, form, etc., were obvious suggestions. The breath also, whose very name to the ancients implied an identity with the life or soul, was nothing but air; and the identification of Air with Life supplied just that principle of productiveness and movement, which was felt to be necessary in the primal element of being. The process of existence, then, he conceived as consisting in a certain concentration of this diffused life-giving element into more or less solidified forms, and the ultimate separation and expansion of these back into the formless air again. The contrary forces previously used by Anaximander—heat and cold, drought and moisture—are with Anaximenes also the agencies which institute these changes.

This is pretty nearly all that we know of Anaximenes. So far as the few known facts reveal him, we can hardly say that except as supplying a step towards the completer development of the *motive* idea in being, he greatly adds to the chain of progressive thought.

IV. HERACLITUS.—Although not a native of Miletus, but of Ephesus, Heraclitus, both by his nationality as an Ionian and by his position in the development of philosophic conceptions, falls naturally to be classed with the philosophers of Miletus. His period may be given approximately as from about 560 to 500 B.C., though others place him a generation later. Few authentic particulars have been preserved of him. We hear of extensive travels, of his return to his native city only to refuse a share in its activities, of his retirement to a hermit's life. He seems to have formed a contrast to the preceding philosophers in his greater detachment from the ordinary interests of civic existence; and much in his teaching suggests the ascetic if not the misanthrope. He received the nickname of 'The Obscure,' from the studied mystery in which he was supposed to involve his teaching. He wrote not for the vulgar, but for the gifted few. 'Much learning makes not wise' was the motto of his work; the man of gift, of insight, that man is better than ten thousand. He was savage in his criticism of other writers, even the greatest. Homer, he said, and Archilochus too, deserved to be hooted from the platform and thrashed. Even the main purport of his writings was differently interpreted. Some named his work 'The Muses,' as though it were chiefly a poetic vision; others named it 'The sure Steersman to the Goal of Life'; others, more prosaically, 'A Treatise of Nature.'

The fundamental principle or fact of being Heraclitus formulated in the famous dictum, 'All things pass.' In the eternal flux or flow of being consisted its reality; even as in a river the water is ever changing, and the river exists as a river only in virtue of this continual change; or as in a living body, wherein while there is life there is no stability or fixedness; stability and fixedness are the attributes of the unreal image of life, not of life itself. Thus, as will be observed, from the *material* basis of being as conceived by Thales, with only a very vague conception of the counter-principle of movement, philosophy has wheeled round in Heraclitus to the other extreme; he finds his permanent element in the negation of permanence; being or reality consists in never 'being' but always 'becoming,' not in stability but in change.

This eternal movement he pictures elsewhere as an eternal strife of opposites, whose differences nevertheless consummate themselves in finest harmony. Thus oneness emerges out of multiplicity, multiplicity out of oneness; and the harmony of the universe is of contraries, as of the lyre and the bow. *War* is the father and king and lord of all things. Neither god nor man presided at the creation of anything that is; that which was, is that which is, and that whichever shall be; even an ever-living Fire, ever kindling and ever being extinguished.

Thus in *Fire*, as an image or symbol of the underlying reality of existence, Heraclitus advanced to the furthest limit attainable on physical lines, for the expression of its essentially *motive* character. That this Fire was no more than a symbol, suggested by the special characteristics of fire in nature,—its subtlety, its mobility, its power of penetrating all things and devouring all things, its powers for beneficence in the warmth of living bodies and the life-giving power of the sun,—is seen in the fact that he readily varies his expression for this principle, calling it at times the Thunderbolt, at others the eternal Reason, or Law, or Fate. To his mental view creation was a process eternally in action, the fiery element descending by the law of its being into the cruder forms of water and earth, only to be resolved again by upward process into fire; even as one sees the vapor from the sea ascending and melting into the aether. As a kindred vapor or exhalation he recognized the Soul or Breath for a manifestation of the essential element. It is formless, ever changing with every breath we take, yet it is the constructive and unifying force which keeps the body together, and conditions its life and growth. At this point Heraclitus comes into touch with Anaximenes. In the act of breathing we draw into our own being a portion of the all-pervading vital element of all being; in this universal being we thereby live and move and have our consciousness; the eternal and omnipresent wisdom becomes, through the channels of our senses, and especially through the eyes, in fragments at least our wisdom. In sleep we are not indeed cut off wholly from this wisdom; through our breathing we hold as it were to its root; but of its flower we are then deprived. On awaking again we begin once more to partake according to our full measure of the living thought; even as coals when brought near the fire are themselves made partakers of it, but when taken away again become quenched.

Hence, in so far as man is wise, it is because his spirit is kindled by union with the universal spirit; but there is a baser, or, as Heraclitus termed it, a moister element also in him, which is the element of unreason, as in a drunken man. And thus the trustworthiness or otherwise of the senses, as the channels of communication with the divine, depends on the *dryness* or *moistness*,—or, as we should express it, using, after all, only another metaphor,—on the *elevation* or *baseness* of the spirit that is within. To those whose souls are base and barbarous, the eternal movement, the living fire, is invisible; and thus what they do see is nothing but death. Immersed in the mere appearances of things and their supposed stability, they, whether sleeping or waking, behold only dead forms; their spirits are dead.

For the guidance of life there is no law but the common sense, which is the union of those fragmentary perceptions of eternal law, which individual men attain, in so far as their spirits are dry and pure. Of absolute knowledge human nature is not capable, but only the Divine. To the Eternal, therefore, alone all things are good and beautiful and just, because to Him alone do things appear in their totality. To the human partial reason some things are unjust and others just. Hence life, by reason of the limitations involved in it, he sometimes spoke of as the death of the soul, and death as the renewal of its life. And so, in the great events of man's life and in the small, as in the mighty circle of the heavens, good and evil, life and death, growth and decay, are but the systole and diastole, the outward and inward pulsation, of an eternal good, an eternal harmony. Day and night, winter and summer, war and peace, satiety and hunger—each conditions the other, all are part of God. It is sickness that makes health good and sweet, hunger that gives its pleasure to feeding, weariness that makes sleep a good.

This vision of existence in its eternal flux and interchange, seems to have inspired Heraclitus with a contemplative melancholy. In the traditions of later times he was known as the *weeping* philosopher. Lucian represents him as saying, "To me it is a sorrow that there is nothing fixed or secure, and that all things are thrown confusedly together, so that pleasure and pain, knowledge and ignorance, the great and the small, are the same, ever circling round and passing one into the other in the sport of time." "Time," he says elsewhere, "is like a child that plays with the dice." The highest good, therefore, for mortals is that clarity of perception in respect of oneself and all that is, whereby we shall learn to apprehend somewhat of the eternal unity and harmony, that underlies the good and evil of time, the shock and stress of circumstance and place. The highest virtue for man is a placid and a quiet constancy, whatever the changes and chances of life may bring. It is the pantheistic apathy.

The sadder note of humanity, the note of Euripides and at times of Sophocles, the note of Dante and of the *Tempest* of Shakespeare, of Shelley and Arnold and

Carlyle,—this note we hear thus early and thus clear, in the dim and distant utterances of Heraclitus. The mystery of existence, the unreality of what seems most real, the intangibility and evanescence of all things earthly,—these thoughts obscurely echoing to us across the ages from Heraclitus, have remained, and always will remain, among the deepest and most insistent of the world's thoughts, in its sincerest moments and in its greatest thinkers.

CHAPTER III

PYTHAGORAS AND THE PYTHAGOREANS

The Pythagorean Brotherhood—Number the master—God the soul of the world—Music and morals

The birthplace of Pythagoras is uncertain. He is generally called the Samian, and we know, at all events, that he lived for some time in that island, during or immediately before the famous tyranny of Polycrates. All manner of legends are told of the travels of Pythagoras to Egypt, Chaldaea, Phoenicia, and even to India. Others tell of a mysterious initiation at the sacred cave of Jupiter in Crete, and of a similar ceremony at the Delphic oracle. What is certain is that at some date towards the end of the sixth century B.C. he removed to Southern Italy, which was then extensively colonized by Greeks, and that there he became a great philosophic teacher, and ultimately even a predominating political influence.

He instituted a school in the strictest sense, with its various grades of learners, subject for years to a vow of silence, holding all things in common, and admitted, according to their approved fitness, to successive revelations of the true doctrine of the Master. Those in the lower grades were called Listeners; those in the higher, Mathematicians or Students; those in the most advanced stage, Physicists or Philosophers. With the political relations of the school we need not here concern ourselves. In Crotona and many other Greek cities in Italy Pythagoreans became a predominant aristocracy, who, having learned obedience under their master, applied what they had learned in an anti-democratic policy of government. This lasted for some thirty years, but ultimately democracy gained the day, and Pythagoreanism as a political power was violently rooted out.

Returning to the philosophy of Pythagoras, in its relation to the general development of Greek theory, we may note, to begin with, that it is not necessary, or perhaps possible, to disentangle the theory of Pythagoras himself from that of his followers, Philolaus and others. The teaching was largely oral, and was developed by successive leaders of the school. The doctrine, therefore, is generally spoken of as that, not of Pythagoras, but of the Pythagoreans. Nor can we fix for certain on one fundamental conception, upon which the whole structure of their doctrine was built.

One dictum we may start with because of its analogies with what has been said of the earlier philosophies. The universe, said the Pythagoreans, was constituted of *indefinites* and *definers*, *i.e.* of that which has no character, but has infinite capacities of taking a character; and secondly, of things or forces which impose a character upon this. Out of the combination of these two elements or principles all knowable existences come into being. "All things," they said, "as known have *Number*; and this number has two natures, the Odd and the Even; the known thing is the Odd-Even or union of the two."

By a curious and somewhat fanciful development of this conception the Pythagoreans drew up two parallel columns of antithetical principles in nature, ten in each, thus:—

Definite Indefinite

Odd	Even
One	Many
Right	Left
Male	Female
Steadfast	Moving
Straight	Bent
Light	Dark
Good	Evil
Four Square Irregular	

Looking down these two lists we shall see that the first covers various aspects of what is conceived as the ordering, defining, formative principle in nature; and that the second in like manner comprises various aspects of the unordered, neutral, passive, or disorganized element or principle; the first, to adopt a later method of expression, is *Form*, the second *Matter*. How this antithesis was worked out by Plato and Aristotle we shall see later on.

While, in a sense, then, even the indefinite has number, inasmuch as it is capable of having number or order imposed upon it (and only in so far as it has this imposed upon it, does it become knowable or intelligible), yet, as a positive factor, Number belongs only to the first class; as such it is the source of all knowledge and of all good. In reality the Pythagoreans had not got any further by this representation of nature than was reached, for example, by Anaximander, and still more definitely by Heraclitus, when they posited an Indefinite or Infinite principle in nature which by the clash of innate antagonisms developed into a knowable universe. But one can easily imagine that once the idea of Number became associated with that of the knowable in things, a wide field of detailed development and experiment, so to speak, in the arcana of nature, seemed to be opened. Every arithmetical or geometrical theorem became in this view another window giving light into the secret heart of things. Number became a kind of god, a revealer; and the philosophy of number a kind of religion or mystery. And this is why the second grade of disciples were called Mathematicians; mathematics was the essential preparation for and initiation into philosophy.

Whether that which truly exists was actually identical with Number or Numbers, or whether it was something different from Number, but had a certain relation to Number; whether if there were such a relation, this was merely a relation of analogy or of conformability, or whether Number were something actually embodied in that which truly exists—these were speculative questions which were variously answered by various teachers, and which probably interested the later more than the earlier leaders of the school.

A further question arose: Assuming that ultimately the elements of knowable existence are but two, the One or Definite, and the Manifold or Indefinite, it was argued by some that there must be some third or higher principle governing the relations of these; there must be some law or harmony which shall render their intelligible union possible. This principle of union was God, ever-living, ever One, eternal, immovable, self-identical. This was the supreme reality, the Odd-Even or Many in One, One in Many, in whom was gathered up, as in an eternal harmony, all the contrarieties of lower existence. Through the interchange and intergrowth of these contrarieties God realizes Himself; the universe in its evolution is the self-picturing of God. God is diffused as the seminal principle throughout the universe; He is the Soul of the world, and the world itself is God in process. The world, therefore, is in a sense a living creature. At its heart and circumference are purest fire; between these circle the sun, the moon, and the five planets, whose ordered movements, as of seven chords, produce an eternal music, the 'Music of the Spheres.' Earth, too, like the planets, is a celestial body, moving like them around the central fire.

By analogy with this conception of the universe as the realization of God, so also the body, whether of man or of any creature, is the realization for the time being of a soul. Without the body and the life of the body, that soul were a blind and fleeting ghost. Of such unrealized souls there are many in various degrees and states; the whole air indeed is full of spirits, who are the causes of dreams and omens.

Thus the change and flux that are visible in all else are visible also in the relations of soul and body. Multitudes of fleeting ghosts or spirits are continually seeking realization through union with bodies, passing at birth into this one and that, and at death issuing forth again into the void. Like wax which takes now one impression now another, yet remains in itself ever the same, so souls vary in the outward form that envelops and realizes them. In this bodily life, the Pythagoreans are elsewhere described as saying, we are as it were in bonds or in a prison, whence we may not justly go forth till the Lord calls us. This idea Cicero mistranslated with a truly Roman fitness: according to him they taught that in this life we are as sentinels at our post, who may not quit it till our Commander orders.

On the one hand, therefore, the union of soul with body was necessary for the realization of the former ((Greek) *soma, body*, being as it were (Greek) *sema, expression*), even as the reality of God was not in the Odd or Eternal Unity, but in the Odd-Even, the Unity in Multiplicity. On the other hand this union implied a certain loss or degradation. In other words, in so far as the soul became realized it also became corporatized, subject to the influence of passion and change. In a sense therefore the soul as realized was double; in itself it partook of the eternal reason, as associated with body it belonged to the realm of unreason.

This disruption of the soul into two the Pythagoreans naturally developed in time into a threefold division, *pure thought, perception,* and *desire*; or even more nearly approaching the Platonic division, they divided it into *reason, passion,* and *desire.* But the later developments were largely influenced by Platonic and other doctrines, and need not be further followed here.

Music had great attractions for Pythagoras, not only for its soothing and refining effects, but for the intellectual interest of its numerical relations. Reference has already been made to their quaint doctrine of the music of the spheres; and the same idea of rhythmic harmony pervaded the whole system. The life of the soul was a harmony; the virtues were perfect numbers; and the influence of music on the soul was only one instance among many of the harmonious relations of things throughout the universe. Thus we have Pythagoras described as soothing mental afflictions, and bodily ones also, by rhythmic measure and by song. With the morning's dawn he would be astir, harmonizing his own spirit to his lyre, and chanting ancient hymns of the Cretan Thales, of Homer, and of Hesiod, till all the tremors of his soul were calmed and still.

Night and morning also he prescribed for himself and his followers an examination, as it were a *tuning* and testing of oneself. At these times especially was it meet for us to take account of our soul and its doings; in the evening to ask, "Wherein have I transgressed? What done? What failed to do?" In the morning, "What must I do? Wherein repair past days' forgetfulness?"

But the first duty of all was truth,—truth to one's own highest, truth to the highest beyond us. Through truth alone could the soul approach the divine. Falsehood was of the earth; the real life of the soul must be in harmony with the heavenly and eternal verities.

Pythagoreanism remained a power for centuries throughout the Greek world and beyond. All subsequent philosophies borrowed from it, as it in its later developments borrowed from them; and thus along with them it formed the mind of the world, for further apprehensions, and yet more authentic revelations, of divine order and moral excellence.

CHAPTER IV

THE ELEATICS

God and nature—Knowledge and opinion—Being and evolution—Love the creator—The modern egotism

I. XENOPHANES.—Xenophanes was a native of Colophon, one of the Ionian cities of Asia Minor, but having been forced at the age of twenty-five to leave his native city owing to some political revolution, he wandered to various cities of Greece, and ultimately to Zancle and Catana, Ionian colonies in Sicily, and thence to Elea or Velia, a Greek city on the coast of Italy. This city had, like Miletus, reached a high pitch of commercial prosperity, and like it also became a centre of philosophic teaching. For there Xenophanes remained and founded a school, so that he and his successors received the name of Eleatics. His date is uncertain; but he seems to have been contemporary with Anaximander and Pythagoras, and to have had some knowledge of the doctrine of both. He wrote in various poetic measures, using against the poets, and especially against Homer and Hesiod, their own weapons, to denounce their anthropomorphic theology. If oxen or lions had hands, he said, they would have fashioned gods after their likeness which would have been as authentic as Homer's. As against these poets, and the popular mythology, he insisted that God must be one, eternal, incorporeal, without beginning or ending. As Aristotle strikingly expresses it, "He looked forth over the whole heavens and said that God is one, that that which is one is God." The favorite antitheses of his time, the definite and the indefinite, movable and immovable, change-producing and by change produced—these and such as these, he maintained, were inapplicable to the eternally and essentially existent. In this there was no partition of organs or faculties, no variation or shadow of turning; the Eternal Being was like a sphere, everywhere equal; everywhere self-identical.

His proof of this was a logical one; the absolutely self-existent could not be thought in conjunction with attributes which either admitted any external influencing Him, or any external influenced by Him. The prevailing dualism he considered to be, as an ultimate theory of the universe, unthinkable and therefore false. Outside the Self-existent there could be no second self-existent, otherwise each would be conditioned by the existence of the other, and the Self-existent would be gone. Anything different from the Self-existent must be of the non-existent, *i.e.* must be nothing.

One can easily see in these discussions some adumbration of many theological or metaphysical difficulties of later times, as of the origin of evil, of freewill in man, of the relation of the created world to its Creator. If these problems cannot be said to be solved yet, we need not be surprised that Xenophanes did not solve them. He was content to emphasize that which seemed to him to be necessary and true, that God was God, and not either a partner with, or a function of, matter.

At the same time he recognized a world of phenomena, or, as he expressed it, a world of guesswork or opinion ((Greek) *doxa*). As to the origin of things within this sphere he was ready enough to borrow from the speculations of his predecessors. Earth and water are the sources from which we spring; and he imagined a time when there was neither sea nor land, but an all-pervading slough and slime; nay, many such periods of inundation and emergence had been, hence the sea-shells on the tops of mountains and the fossils in the rocks. Air and fire also as agencies of change are sometimes referred to by him; anticipations in fact are visible of the fourfold classification of the elements which was formally made by some of his successors.

II. PARMENIDES.—The pupil and successor of Xenophanes was PARMENIDES, a native of Elea. In a celebrated dialogue of Plato bearing the name of this philosopher he is described as visiting Socrates when the latter was very young. "He was then already advanced in years, very hoary, yet noble to look upon, in years some sixty and five." Socrates was born about 479 B.C. The birth of Parmenides might therefore, if this indication be authentic, be about 520. He was of a wealthy and noble family, and able therefore to devote himself to a learned leisure. Like his master he expounded his views in verse, and fragments of his poem of considerable length and importance have been preserved. The title of the work was *Peri Phueos—Of Nature.*

The exordium of the poem is one of some grandeur. The poet describes himself as soaring aloft to the sanctuary of wisdom where it is set in highest aether, the daughters of the Sun being his guides; under whose leading having traversed the path of perpetual day and at length attained the temple of the goddess, he from her lips received instruction in the eternal verities, and had shown to him the deceptive guesses of mortals. "'Tis for thee," she says, "to hear of both,—to have disclosed to thee on the one hand the sure heart of convincing verity, on the other hand the guesses of mortals wherein is no ascertainment. Nevertheless thou shalt learn of these also, that having gone through them all thou may'st see by what unsureness of path must he go who goeth the way of opinion. From such a way of searching restrain thou thy thought, and let not the much-experimenting habit force thee along the path wherein thou must use thine eye, yet being sightless, and the ear with its clamorous buzzings, and the chattering tongue. 'Tis by Reason that thou must in lengthened trial judge what I shall say to thee."

Thus, like Xenophanes, Parmenides draws a deep division between the world of reason and the world of sensation, between probative argument and the guess-work of sense-impressions. The former is the world of Being, the world of that which truly is, self-existent, uncreated, unending, unmoved, unchanging, ever self-poised and self-sufficient, like a sphere. Knowledge is of this, and of this only, and as such, knowledge is identical with its object; for outside this known reality there is nothing. In other words, Knowledge can only be of that which is, and that which is alone can know. All things which mortals have imagined to be realities are but words; as of the birth and death of things, of things which were and have ceased to be, of here and there, of now and then.

It is obvious enough that in all this, and in much more to the same effect reiterated throughout the poem, we have no more than a statement, in various forms of negation, of the inconceivability by human reason of that passage from *being* as such, to that world of phenomena which is now, but was not before, and will cease to be,—from *being* to *becoming*, from eternity to time, from the infinite to the finite (or, as Parmenides preferred to call it, from the perfect to the imperfect, the definite to the indefinite). In all this Parmenides was not contradicting such observed facts as generation, or motion, or life, or death; he was talking of a world which has nothing to do with observation; he was endeavoring to grasp what was assumed or necessarily implied as a prior condition of observation, or of a world to observe.

What he and his school seem to have felt was that there was a danger in all this talk of water or air or other material symbol, or even of the *indefinite* or *characterless* as the original of all,—the danger, namely, that one should lose sight of the idea of law, of rationality, of eternal self-centred force, and so be carried away by some vision of a gradual process of evolution from mere emptiness to fullness of being. Such a position would be not dissimilar to that of many would-be metaphysicians among evolutionists, who, not content with the doctrine of evolution as a theory in science, an ordered and organizing view of observed facts, will try to elevate it into a vision of what is, and alone is, behind the observed facts. They fail to see that the more blind, the more accidental, so to speak, the process of differentiation may be; the more it is shown that the struggle for existence drives the wheels of progress along the lines of least resistance by the most commonplace of mechanical necessities, in the same proportion must a law be posited behind all this process, a reason in nature which gathers up the beginning and the ending. The protoplasmic cell which the imagination of evolutionists places at the beginning of time as the starting-point of this mighty process is not merely this or that, has not merely this or that quality or possibility, it *is*; and in the power of that little word is enclosed a whole world of thought, which is there at the first, remains there all through the evolutions of the protoplasm, will be there when these are done, is in fact independent of time and space, has nothing to do with such distinctions, expresses rather their ultimate unreality. So far then as Parmenides and his school kept a firm grip on this other-world aspect of nature as implied even in the simple word *is*, or *be*, so far they did good service in the process of the world's thought. On the other hand, he and they were naturally enough disinclined, as we all are disinclined, to remain in the merely or mainly negative or defensive. He would not lose his grip of heaven and eternity, but he would fain know the secrets of earth and time as well. And hence was fashioned the second part of his poem, in which he expounds his theory of the world of opinion, or guess-work, or observation.

In this world he found two originative principles at work, one pertaining to light and heat, the other to darkness and cold. From the union of these two principles all observable things in creation come, and over this union a God-given power presides, whose name is Love. Of these two principles, the bright one being analogous to *Fire*, the dark one to *Earth*, he considered the former to be the male or formative element, the latter the female or passive element; the former therefore had analogies to Being as such, the latter to Non-being. The heavenly existences, the sun, the moon, the stars, are of pure Fire, have therefore an eternal and unchangeable being; they are on the extremist verge of the universe, and corresponding to them at the centre is another fiery sphere, which, itself unmoved, is the cause of all motion and generation in the mixed region between. The motive and procreative power, sometimes called Love, is at other times called by Parmenides Necessity, Bearer of the Keys, Justice, Ruler, etc.

But while in so far as there was union in the production of man or any other creature, the presiding genius might be symbolized as *Love*; on the other hand, since this union was a union of opposites (Light and Dark), *Discord* or *Strife* also had her say in the union. Thus the nature and character in every creature was the resultant of two antagonistic forces, and depended for its particular excellence or defect on the proportions in which these two elements—the light and the dark, the fiery and the earthy—had been commingled.

No character in Greek antiquity, at least in the succession of philosophic teachers, held a more honored position than Parmenides. He was looked on with almost superstitious reverence by his fellow-countrymen. Plato speaks of him as his "Father Parmenides," whom he "revered and honored more than all the other philosophers together." To quote Professor Jowett in his introduction to Plato's dialogue *Parmenides*, he was "the founder of idealism and also of dialectic, or in modern phraseology, of metaphysics and of logic." Of the logical aspect of his teaching we shall see a fuller exemplification in his pupil and successor Zeno; of his metaphysics, by way of summing up what has been already said, it may be remarked that its substantial excellence consists in the perfect clearness and precision with which Parmenides enunciated as fundamental in any theory of the knowable universe the priority of Existence itself, not in time merely or chiefly, but as a condition of having any problem to inquire into. He practically admits that he does not see how to bridge over the partition between Existence in itself and the changeful, temporary, existing things which the senses give us notions of. But whatever the connection may be, if there is a connection, he is convinced that nothing would be more absurd than to make the data of sense in any way or degree the measure of the reality of existence, or the source from which existence itself comes into being.

On this serenely impersonal position he took his stand; we find little or nothing of the querulous personal note so characteristic of much modern philosophy. We never find him asking, "What is to become of *me* in all this?" "What is *my* position with regard to this eternally-existing reality?"

Of course this is not exclusively a characteristic of Parmenides, but of the time. The idea of personal relation to an eternal Rewarder was only vaguely held in historical times in Greece. The conception of personal immortality was a mere pious opinion, a doctrine whispered here and there in secret mystery; it was not an influential force on men's motives or actions. Thought was still occupied with the wider universe, the heavens and their starry wonders, and the strange phenomena of law in nature. In the succession of the seasons, the rising and setting, the fixities and aberrations, of the heavenly bodies, in the mysteries of coming into being and passing out of it, in these and other similar marvels, and in the thoughts which they evoked, a whole and ample world seemed open for inquiry. Men and their fate were interesting enough to men, but as yet the egotism of man had not attempted to isolate his destiny from the general problem of nature. To the *crux* of philosophy as it appeared to Parmenides in the relation of being as such to things which seem to be, modernism has appended a sort of corollary, in the relation of being as such to *my* being. Till the second question was raised its answer, of course, could not be attempted. But all those who in modern times have said with Tennyson—

Thou wilt not leave us in the dust:
Thou madest man, he knows not why;
He thinks he was not made to die;
And Thou hast made him: Thou art just,

may recognize in Parmenides a pioneer for them. Without knowing it, he was fighting the battle of personality in man, as well as that of reality in nature.

CHAPTER V

THE ELEATICS (*concluded*)

Zeno's dialectic—Achilles and the tortoise—The dilemma of being—The all a sphere—The dilemmas of experience

III. ZENO.—The third head of the Eleatic school was ZENO. He is described by Plato in the *Parmenides* as accompanying his master to Athens on the visit already referred to, and as being then "nearly forty years of age, of a noble figure and fair aspect." In personal character he was a worthy pupil of his master, being, like him, a devoted patriot. He is even said to have fallen a victim to his patriotism, and to have suffered bravely the extremist tortures at the hands of a tyrant Nearchus rather than betray his country.

His philosophic position was a very simple one. He had nothing to add to or to vary in the doctrine of Parmenides. His function was primarily that of an expositor and defender of that doctrine, and his particular pre-eminence consists in the ingenuity of his dialectic resources of defense. He is in fact pronounced by Aristotle to have been the inventor of dialectic or systematic logic. The relation of the two is humorously expressed thus by Plato (Jowett, *Plato*, vol. iv. p. 128); "I see, Parmenides, said Socrates, that Zeno is your second self in his writings too; he puts what you say in another way, and would fain deceive us into believing that he is telling us what is new. For you, in your poems, say, All is one, and of this you adduce excellent proofs; and he, on the other hand, says, There is no many; and on behalf of this he offers overwhelming evidence." To this Zeno replies, admitting the fact, and adds: "These writings of mine were meant to protect the arguments of Parmenides against those who scoff at him, and show the many ridiculous and contradictory results which they suppose to follow from the affirmation of the One. My answer is an address to the partisans of the many, whose attack I return with interest by retorting upon them that their hypothesis of the being of many if carried out appears in a still more ridiculous light than the hypothesis of the being of one."

The arguments of Zeno may therefore be regarded as strictly arguments *in kind*; quibbles if you please, but in answer to quibbles. The secret of his method was what Aristotle calls Dichotomy—that is, he put side by side two contradictory propositions with respect to any particular supposed real thing in experience, and then proceeded to show that both these contradictories alike imply what is inconceivable. Thus "a thing must consist either of a finite number of parts or an infinite number." Assume the number of parts to be finite. Between them there must either be something or nothing. If there is something between them, then the whole consists of more parts than it consists of. If there is nothing between them, then they are not separated, therefore they are not parts; therefore the whole has no parts at all; therefore it is nothing. If, on the other hand, the number of parts is infinite, then, the same kind of argument being applied, the magnitude of the whole is by infinite successive positing of intervening parts shown to be infinite; therefore this one thing, being infinitely large, is everything.

Take, again, any supposed fact, as that an arrow moves. An arrow cannot move except in space. It cannot move in space without being in space. At any moment of its supposed motion it must be in a particular space. Being in that space, it must at the time during which it is in it be at rest. But the total time of its supposed motion is made up of the moments composing that time, and to each of these moments the same argument applies; therefore either the arrow never was anywhere, or it always was at rest.

Or, again, take objects moving at unequal rates, as Achilles and a tortoise. Let the tortoise have a start of any given length, then Achilles, however much he excel in speed, will never overtake the tortoise. For, while Achilles has passed over the originally intervening space, the tortoise will have passed over a certain space, and when Achilles has passed over this second space the tortoise will have again passed over some space, and so on *ad infinitum*; therefore in an infinite time there must always be a space, though infinitely diminishing, between the tortoise and Achilles, *i.e.* the tortoise must always be at least a little in front.

These will be sufficient to show the kind of arguments employed by Zeno. In themselves they are of no utility, and Zeno never pretended that they had any. But as against those who denied that existence as such was a datum independent of experience, something different from a mere sum of isolated things, his arguments were not only effective, but substantial. The whole modern sensational or experiential school, who derive our 'abstract ideas,' as they are called, from 'phenomena' or 'sensation,' manifest the same impatience of any analysis of what they mean by phenomena or sensation, as no doubt Zeno's opponents manifested of his analyses. As in criticizing the one, modern critics are ready with their answer that Zeno's quibbles are simply "a play of words on the well-known properties of infinities," so they are quick to tell us that sensation is an "affection of the sentient organism"; ignoring in the first case the prior question where the idea of infinity came from, and in the second, where the idea of a sentient organism came from.

Indirectly, as we shall see, Zeno had a great effect on subsequent philosophies by the development of a process of ingenious verbal distinction, which in the hands of so-called sophists and others became a weapon of considerable, if temporary, power.

IV. MELISSUS.—The fourth and last of the Eleatic philosophers was Melissus, a native of Samos. His date may be fixed as about 440 B.C. He took an active part in the politics of his native country, and on one occasion was commander of the Samian fleet in a victorious engagement with the Athenians, when Samos was being besieged by Pericles. He belongs to the Eleatic school in respect of doctrine and method, but we have no evidence of his ever having resided at Elea, nor any reference to his connection with the philosophers there, except the statement that he was a pupil of Parmenides. He developed very fully what is technically called in the science of Logic the *Dilemma*. Thus, for example, he begins his treatise *On Existence* or *On Nature* thus: "If nothing exists, then there is nothing for us to talk about. But if there is such a thing as existence it must either come into being or be ever-existing. If it come into being, it must come from the existing or the non-existing. Now that anything which exists, above all, that which is absolutely existent, should come from what is not, is impossible. Nor can it come from that which is. For then it would be already, and would not come into being. That which exists, therefore, comes not into being; it must therefore be ever-existing."

By similar treatment of other conceivable alternatives he proceeds to show that as the existent had no beginning so it can have no ending in time. From this, by a curious transition which Aristotle quotes as an example of loose reasoning, he concludes that the existent can have no limit in space either. As being thus unlimited it must be one, therefore immovable (there being nothing else into which it can move or change), and therefore always self-identical in extent and character. It cannot, therefore, have anybody, for body has parts and is not therefore one.

Being incapable of change one might perhaps conclude that the absolutely existing being is incapable of any mental activity or consciousness. We have no authority for assuming that Melissus came to this conclusion; but there is a curious remark of Aristotle's respecting this and previous philosophers of the school which certain critics have made to bear some such interpretation. He says: "Parmenides seems to hold by a Unity in thought, Melissus by a Material unity. Hence the first defined the One as limited, the second declared it to be unlimited. Xenophanes made no clear statement on this question; he simply, gazing up to the arch of heaven, declared, The One is God."

But the difference between Melissus and his master can hardly be said to be a difference of doctrine; point for point, they are identical. The difference is a difference of vision or mental picture as to this mighty All which is One. Melissus, so to speak, places himself at the centre of this Universal being, and sees it stretching out infinitely, unendingly, in space and in time. Its oneness comes to him as the *sum* of these infinities. Parmenides, on the other hand, sees all these endless immensities as related to a centre; he, so to speak, enfolds them all in the grasp of his unifying thought, and as thus equally and necessarily related to a central unity he pronounces the All a sphere, and therefore limited. The two doctrines, antithetical in terms, are identical in fact. The absolutely unlimited and the absolutely self-limited are only two ways of saying the same thing.

This difference of view or vision Aristotle in the passage quoted expresses as a difference between *thought* ((Greek) *logos*) and *matter* ((Greek) *hule*). This is just a form of his own radical distinction between Essence and Difference, Form and Matter, of which much will be said later on. It is like the difference between Deduction and Induction; in the first you start from the universal and see within it the particulars; in the second you start from the particulars and gather them into completeness and reality in a universal. The substance remains the same, only the point of view is different. To put the matter in modern mathematical form, one might say, The universe is to be conceived as a *sphere* (Parmenides) of *infinite radius* (Melissus). Aristotle is not blaming Melissus or praising Parmenides. As for Xenophanes, Aristotle after his manner finds in him the potentiality of both. He is prior both to the process of thought from universal to particular, and to that from particular to universal. He does not argue at all; his function is Intuition. "He looks out on the mighty sky, and says, The One is God."

Melissus applied the results of his analysis in an interesting way to the question already raised by his predecessors, of the trustworthiness of sensation. His argument is as follows: "If there were many real existences, to each of them the same reasoning must apply as I have already used with reference to the one existence. That is to say, if earth really exists, and water and air and iron and gold and fire and things living and things dead; and black and white, and all the various things whose reality men ordinarily assume,—if all these really exist, and our sight and our hearing give us *facts*, then each of these as really existing must be what we concluded the one existence must be; among other things, each must be unchangeable, and can never become other than it really is. But assuming that sight and hearing and apprehension are true, we find the cold becoming hot and the hot becoming cold; the hard changes to soft, the soft to hard; the living thing dies; and from that which is not living, a living thing comes into being; in short, everything changes, and what now is in no way resembles what was. It follows therefore that we neither see nor apprehend realities.

"In fact we cannot pay the slightest regard to experience without being landed in self-contradictions. We assume that there are all sorts of really existing things, having a permanence both of form and power, and yet we imagine these very things altering and changing according to what we from time to time see about them. If they were realities as we first perceived them, our sight must now be wrong. For if they were real, they could not change. Nothing can be stronger than reality. Whereas to suppose it changed, we must affirm that the real has ceased to be, and that that which was not has displaced it."

To Melissus therefore, as to his predecessors, the world of sense was a world of illusion; the very first principles or assumptions of which, as of the truthfulness of the senses and the reality of the various objects which we see, are unthinkable and absurd.

The weakness as well as the strength of the Eleatic position consisted in its purely negative and critical attitude. The assumptions of ordinary life and experience could not stand for a moment when assailed in detail by their subtle analysis. So-called facts were like a world of ghosts, which the sword of truth passed through without resistance. But somehow the sword might pierce them through and through, and show by all manner of arguments their unsubstantiality, but there they were still thronging about the philosopher and refusing to be gone. The world of sense might be only illusion, but there the illusion was. You could not lay it or exorcise it by calling it illusion or opinion. What was this opinion? What was the nature of its subject matter? How did it operate? And if its results were not true or real, what was their nature? These were questions which still remained when the analysis of the idea of absolute existence had been pushed to its completion. These were the questions which the next school of philosophy attempted to answer. After the Idealists, the Realists; after the philosophy of mind, the philosophy of matter.

CHAPTER VI

THE ATOMISTS

Anaxagoras and the cosmos—Mind in nature—The seeds of existence

I. ANAXAGORAS.—Anaxagoras was born at Clazomenae, a city of Ionia, about the year 500 B.C. At the age of twenty he removed to Athens, of which city Clazomenae was for some time a dependency. This step on his part may have been connected with the circumstances attending the great invasion of Greece by Xerxes in the year 480. For Xerxes drew a large contingent of his army from the Ionian cities which he had subdued, and many who were unwilling to serve against their mother-country may have taken refuge about that time in Athens. At Athens he resided for nearly fifty years, and during that period became the friend and teacher of many eminent men, among the rest of Pericles, the great Athenian statesman, and of Euripides, the dramatist. Like most of the Ionian philosophers he had a taste for mathematics and astronomy, as well as for certain practical applications of mathematics. Among other books he is said to have written a treatise on the art of scene-designing for the stage, possibly to oblige his friend and pupil Euripides. In his case, as in that of his predecessors, only fragments of his philosophic writings have been preserved, and the connection of certain portions of his teaching as they have come down to us remains somewhat uncertain.

With respect to the constitution of the universe we have the following: "Origination and destruction are phrases which are generally misunderstood among the Greeks. Nothing really is originated or destroyed; the only processes which actually take place are combination and separation of elements already existing. These elements we are to conceive as having been in a state of chaos at first, infinite in number and infinitely small, forming in their immobility a confused and characterless unity. About this chaos was spread the air and aether, infinite also in the multitude of their particles, and infinitely extended. Before separation commenced there was no clear color or appearance in anything, whether of moist or dry, of hot or cold, of bright or dark, but only an infinite number of the seeds of things, having concealed in them all manner of forms and colors and savors."

There is a curious resemblance in this to the opening verses of Genesis, "The earth was without form and void, and darkness was upon the face of the deep."

Nor is the next step in his philosophy without its resemblance to that in the Biblical record. As summarised by Diogenes Laertius it takes this form, "All things were as one: then cometh Mind, and by division brought all things into order." "Conceiving," as Aristotle puts it, "that the original elements of things had no power to generate or develop out of themselves things as they exist, philosophers were forced by the facts themselves to seek the immediate cause of this development. They were unable to believe that fire, or earth, or any such principle was adequate to account for the order and beauty visible in the frame of things; nor did they think it possible to attribute these to mere innate necessity or chance. *One* (Anaxagoras) observing how in living creatures Mind is the ordering force, declared that in nature also this must be the cause of order and beauty, and in so declaring he seemed, when compared with those before him, as one sober amidst a crowd of babblers."

Elsewhere, however, Aristotle modifies this commendation. "Anaxagoras," he says, "uses Mind only as a kind of last resort, dragging it in when he fails otherwise to account for a phenomenon, but never thinking of it else." And in the *Phaedo* Plato makes Socrates speak of the high hopes with which he had taken to the works of Anaxagoras, and how grievously he had been disappointed. "As I proceeded," he says, "I found my philosopher altogether forsaking Mind or any other principle of order, and having recourse to air, and aether, and water, and other eccentricities."

Anaxagoras, then, at least on this side of his teaching, must be considered rather as the author of a phrase than as the founder of a philosophy. The phrase remained, and had a profound influence on subsequent philosophies, but in his own hands it was little more than a dead letter. His immediate interest was rather in the variety of phenomena than in their conceived principle of unity; he is theoretically, perhaps, 'on the side of the angels,' in practice he is a materialist.

Mind he conceived as something apart, sitting throned like Zeus upon the heights, giving doubtless the first impulse to the movement of things, but leaving them for the rest to their own inherent tendencies. As distinguished from them it was, he conceived, the one thing which was absolutely pure and unmixed. All things else had intermixture with every other, the mixtures increasing in complexity towards the centre of things. On the outmost verge were distributed the finest and least complex forms of things—the sun, the moon, the stars; the more dense gathering together, to form as it were in the centre of the vortex, the earth and its manifold existences. By the intermixture of air and earth and water, containing in themselves the infinitely varied seeds of things, plants and animals were developed. The seeds themselves are too minute to be apprehended by the senses, but we can divine their character by the various characters of the visible things themselves, each of these having a necessary correspondence with the nature of the seeds from which they respectively were formed.

Thus for a true apprehension of things sensation and reason are both necessary—sensation to certify to the apparent characters of objects, reason to pass from these to the nature of the invisible seeds or atoms which cause those characters. Taken by themselves our sensations are false, inasmuch as they give us only combined impressions, yet they are a necessary stage towards the truth, as providing the materials which reason must separate into their real elements.

From this brief summary we may gather that Mind was conceived, so to speak, as placed at the *beginning* of existence, inasmuch as it is the first originator of the vortex motions of the atoms or seeds of things; it was conceived also at the *end* of existence as the power which by analysis of the data of sensation goes back through the complexity of actual being to the original unmingled or undeveloped nature of things. But the whole process of nature itself between these limits Anaxagoras conceived as a purely mechanical or at least physical development, the uncertainty of his view as between these two alternative ways of considering it being typified in his use of the two expressions *atoms* and *seeds*. The analogies of this view with those of modern materialism, which finds in the ultimate molecules of matter "the promise and the potency of all life and all existence," need not be here enlarged upon.

After nearly half a century's teaching at Athens Anaxagoras was indicted on a charge of inculcating doctrines subversive of religion. It is obvious enough that his theories left no room for the popular mythology, but the Athenians were not usually very sensitive as to the bearing of mere theories upon their public institutions. It seems probable that the accusation was merely a cloak for political hostility. Anaxagoras was the friend and intimate of Pericles, leader of the democratic party in the state, and the attack upon Anaxagoras was really a political move intended to damage Pericles. As such Pericles himself accepted it, and the trial became a contest of strength, which resulted in a partial success and a partial defeat for both sides. Pericles succeeded in saving his friend's life, but the opposite party obtained a sentence of fine and banishment against him. Anaxagoras retired to Lampsacus, a city on the Hellespont, and there, after some five years, he died.

CHAPTER VII

THE ATOMISTS (*continued*)

Empedocles at Etna—Brief life and scanty vision—The four elements—The philosophy of contradiction—Philosophy a form of poesy—The philosopher a prophet—Sensation through kinship—The whole creation groaneth

II. EMPEDOCLES.—Empedocles was a native of Agrigentum, a Greek colony in Sicily. At the time when he flourished in his native city (circa 440 B.C.) it was one of the wealthiest and most powerful communities in that wealthy and powerful island. It had, however, been infested, like its neighbors, by the designs of tyrants and the dissensions of rival factions. Empedocles was a man of high family, and he exercised the influence which his position and his abilities secured him in promoting and maintaining the liberty of his fellow-countrymen. Partly on this account, partly from a reputation which with or without his own will he acquired for an almost miraculous skill in healing and necromantic arts, Empedocles attained to a position of singular personal power over his contemporaries, and was indeed regarded as semi-divine. His death was hedged about with mystery. According to one story he gave a great feast to his friends and offered a sacrifice; then when his friends went to rest he disappeared, and was no more seen. According to a story less dignified and better known—

Deus immortalis haberi
Dum cupit Empedocles, ardentem frigidus Aetnam
Insiluit. HOR. *Ad Pisones*, 464 *sqq.*

"Eager to be deemed a god, Empedocles coldly threw himself in burning Etna." The fraud, it was said, was detected by one of his shoes being cast up from the crater. Whatever the manner of his end, the Etna story may probably be taken as an ill-natured joke of some skeptic wit; and it is certain that no such story was believed by his fellow-citizens, who rendered in after years divine honors to his name.

Like Xenophanes, Parmenides, and other Graeco-Italian philosophers, he expounded his views in verse; but he reached a poetic excellence unattained by any predecessor. Aristotle characterizes his gift as Homeric, and himself as a master of style, employing freely metaphors and other poetic forms. Lucretius also speaks of him in terms of high admiration (*De Nat. Rer. i. 716 sqq.*): "Foremost among them is Empedocles of Agrigentum, child of the island with the triple capes, a land wondrous deemed in many wise, and worthy to be viewed of all men. Rich it is in all manner of good things, and strong in the might of its men, yet naught within its borders men deem more divine or more wondrous or more dear than her illustrious son. Nay, the songs which issued from his godlike breast are eloquent yet, and expound his findings wondrous well, so that hardly is he thought to have been of mortal clay."

Like the Eleatics he denies that the senses are an absolute test of truth. "For straitened are the powers that have been shed upon our frames, and many the frets that cross us and defeat our care, and short the span of unsatisfying existence wherein 'tis given us to see. Short-lived as a wreath of smoke men rise and fleet away, persuaded but of that alone which each has chanced to light upon, driven hither and thither, and vainly do they pray to find *the whole*. For this men may not see or hear or grasp with the hand of thought." Yet that there is a kind or degree of knowledge possible for man his next words suggest when he continues: "Thou therefore since hither thou hast been borne, hear, and thou shalt learn so much as 'tis given to mortal thought to reach." Then follows an invocation in true Epic style to the "much-wooed white-armed virgin Muse," wherein he prays that "folly and impurity may be far from the lips of him the teacher, and that sending forth her swift-reined chariot from the shrine of Piety, the Muse may grant him to hear so much as is given to mortal hearing."

Then follows a warning uttered by the Muse to her would-be disciple: "Thee the flowers of mortal distinctions shall not seduce to utter in daring of heart more than thou mayest, that thereby thou mightest soar to the highest heights of wisdom. And now behold and see, availing thyself of every device whereby the truth may in each matter be revealed, trusting not more to sight for thy learning than to hearing, nor to hearing with its loud echoings more than to the revelations of the tongue, nor to any one of the many ways whereby there is a path to knowledge. Keep a check on the revelation of the hands also, and apprehend each matter in the way whereby it is made plain to thee."

The correction of the one sense by the others, and of all by reason, this Empedocles deemed the surest road to knowledge. He thus endeavored to hold a middle place between the purely abstract reasoning of the Eleatic philosophy and the unreasoned first guesses of ordinary observation suggested by this or that sense, and chiefly by the eyes. The senses might supply the raw materials of knowledge, unordered, unrelated, nay even chaotic and mutually destructive; but in their contradictions of each other he hoped to find a starting-point for order amidst the seeming chaos; reason should weigh, reason should reject, but reason also should find a residuum of truth.

In our next fragment we have his enunciation in symbolical language of the *four* elements, by him first formulated: "Hear first of all what are the root principles of all things, being four in number,—Zeus the bright shiner (*i.e.* fire), and Hera (air), and life-bearing Aidoneus (earth), and Nestis (water), who with her teardrops waters the fountain of mortality. Hear also this other that I will tell thee. Nothing of all that perisheth ever is created, nothing ever really findeth an end in death. There is naught but a mingling, and a parting again of that which was mingled, and this is what men call a coming into being. Foolish they, for in them is no far-reaching thought, that they should dream that what was not before can be, or that aught which is can utterly perish and die." Thus again Empedocles shows himself an Eclectic; in denying that aught can come into being, he holds with the Eleatics in identifying all seeming creation, and ceasing to be with certain mixtures and separations of matter eternally existing, he links himself rather to the doctrine of Anaxagoras.

These four elements constitute the total *corpus* of the universe, eternal, as a whole unmoved and immovable, perfect like a sphere. But within this sphere-like self-centred All there are eternally proceeding separations and new unions of the elements of things; and every one of these is at once a birth and an infinity of dyings, a dying and an infinity of births. Towards this perpetual life in death, and death in life, two forces work inherent in the universe. One of these he names Love, Friendship, Harmony, Aphrodite goddess of Love, Passion, Joy; the other he calls Hate, Discord, Ares god of War, Envy, Strife. Neither of the one nor of the other may man have apprehension by the senses; they are spiritually discerned; yet of the first men have some adumbration in the creative force within their own members, which they name by the names of Love and Nuptial Joy.

Somewhat prosaically summing up the teaching of Empedocles, Aristotle says that he thus posited *six* first principles in nature—four material, two motive or efficient. And he goes on to remark that in the working out of his theory of nature Empedocles, though using his originative principles more consistently than Anaxagoras used his principle of *Nous* or Thought, not infrequently, nevertheless, resorts to some natural force in the elements themselves, or even to chance or necessity. "Nor," he continues, "has he clearly marked off the functions of his two efficient forces, nay, he has so confounded them that at times it is Discord that through separation leads to new unions, and Love that through union causes diremption of that which was before." At times, too, Empedocles seems to have had a vision of these two forces, not as the counteracting yet co-operative *pulsations*, so to speak, of the universal life, but as rival forces having had in time their periods of alternate supremacy and defeat. While all things were in union under the influence of Love, then was there neither Earth nor Water nor Air nor Fire, much less any of the individual things that in eternal interchange are formed of them; but all was in perfect sphere-like balance, enwrapped in the serenity of an eternal silence. Then came the reign of Discord, whereby war arose in heaven as of the fabled giants, and endless change,—endless birth, and endless death.

These inconsistencies of doctrine, which Aristotle notes as faults in Empedocles, are perhaps rather proofs of the philosophic value of his conceptions. Just as Hegel in modern philosophy could only adequately formulate his conceptions through logical contradictions, so also, perhaps, under the veil of antagonisms of utterance, Empedocles sought to give a fuller vision,—Discord, in his own doctrine, not less than in his conception of nature, being thus the co-worker with Love. The ordinary mind for the ordinary purposes of science seeks exactness of distinction in things, and language, being the creation of ordinary experience, lends itself to such a purpose; the philosophic mind, finding ready to its hand no forms of expression adapted to its conceptions, which have for their final end Union and not Distinction, can only attain its purpose by variety, or even contradictoriness, of representation. Thus to ordinary conception cause must precede effect; to the philosophic mind, dealing as it does with the idea of an organic whole, everything is at once cause and effect, is at once therefore prior to and subsequent to every other, is at once the ruling and the ruled, the conditioning and that which is conditioned.

So, to Empedocles there are four elements, yet in the eternal perfection, the silent reign of Love, there are none of them. There are two forces working upon these and against each other, yet each is like the other either a unifying or a separating force, as one pleases to regard them; and in the eternal silence, the ideal perfectness, there is no warfare at all. There is joy in Love which creates, and in creating destroys; there is joy in the eternal Stillness, nay, this is itself the ultimate joy. There are two forces working, Love and Hate, yet is there but one force, and that force is Necessity. And for final contradiction, the universe is self-balanced, self-conditioned, a perfect sphere; therefore this Necessity is perfect self-realization, and consequently perfect freedom.

The men who have had the profoundest vision of things—Heraclitus, Empedocles, Socrates, Plato, ay, and Aristotle himself when he was the thinker and not the critic; not to speak of the great moderns, whether preachers or philosophers—have none of them been greatly concerned for consistency of expression, for a mere logical self-identity of doctrine. Life in every form, nay, existence in any form, is a union of contradictories, a complex of antagonisms; and the highest and deepest minds are those that are most adequate to have the vision of these antagonisms in their contrariety, and also in their unity; to see and hear as Empedocles did the eternal war and clamor, but to discern also, as he did in it and through it and behind it and about it, the eternal peace and the eternal silence.

Philosophy, in fact, is a form of poesy; it is, if one pleases so to call it, 'fiction founded upon fact.' It is not for that reason the less noble a form of human thought, rather is it the more noble, in the same way as poetry is nobler than mere narrative, and art than representation, and imagination than perception. Philosophy is indeed one of the noblest forms of poetry, because the facts which are its basis are the profoundest, the most eternally interesting, the most universally significant. And not only has it nobility in respect of the greatness of its subject matter, it has also possibilities of an essential truth deeper and more far-reaching and more fruitful than any demonstrative system of fact can have. A great poem or work of art of any kind is an adumbration of truths which transcend any actual fact, and as such it brings us nearer to the underlying fundamentals of reality which all actual occurrences only by accumulation *tend* to realize. Philosophy, then, in so far as it is great, is, like other great art, prophetic in both interpretations of the word, both as expounding the inner truth that is anterior to actuality, and also as anticipating that final realization of all things for which 'the whole creation groaneth.' It is thus at the basis of religion, of art, of morals; it is the accumulated sense of the highest in man with respect to what is greatest and most mysterious in and about him.

The facts, indeed, with which philosophy attempts to deal are so vital and so vast that even the greatest intellects may well stagger occasionally under the burden of their own conceptions of them. To rise to the height of such an argument demands a more than Miltonic imagination; and criticisms directed only at this or that fragment of the whole are as irrelevant, if not as inept, as the criticism of the mathematician directed against *Paradise Lost*, that it 'proved nothing.' The mystery of being and of life, the true purport and reality of this world of which we seem to be a part, and yet of which we seem to have some apprehension as though we were other than a part; the strange problems of creation and change and birth and death, of love and sin and purification; of a heaven dreamt of or believed in, or somehow actually apprehended; of life here, and of an immortality yearned after and hoped for—these problems, these mysteries, no philosophy ever did or ever can empty of their strangeness, or bring down to the level of the commonplace 'certainties' of daily life or of science, which are no more than shadows after all, that seem certainties because of the background of mystery on which they are cast.

But just as an individual is a higher being, a fuller, more truly human creature, when he has got so far removed from the merely animal existence as to realize that there are such problems and mysteries, so also the humanization of the race, the development of its noblest peoples and its noblest literatures, have been conditioned by the successive visions of these mysteries in more and more complex organization by the great philosophers and poets and preachers. The systems of such men may die, but such deaths mean, as Empedocles said of the ordinary deaths of things, only an infinity of new births. Being dead, their systems yet speak in the inherited language and ideas and aspirations and beliefs that form the never-ending, still-renewing material for new philosophies and new faiths. In Thales, Heraclitus, Pythagoras, Parmenides, Empedocles we have been touching hands with an apostolic succession of great men and great thinkers and great poets—men of noble life and lofty thoughts, true prophets and revealers. And the apostolic succession even within the Greek world does not fail for centuries yet.

Passing from the general conceptions of Empedocles to those more particular rationalizations of particular problems which very largely provided the motive of early philosophies, while scientific methods were in an undeveloped and uncritical condition, we may notice such interesting statements as the following: "The earth, which is at the centre of the sphere of the universe, remains firm, because the spin of the universe as a whole keeps it in its place like the water in a spinning cup." He has the same conception of the early condition of the earth as in other cosmogonies. At first it was a chaos of watery slough, which slowly, under the influence of sky and sun, parted off into earth and sea. The sea was the 'sweat' of the earth, and by analogy with the sweat it was salt. The heavens, on the other hand, were formed of air and fire, and the sun was, as it were, a speculum at which the effulgence and the heat of the whole heavens concentrated. But that the aether and the fire had not been fully separated from earth and water he held to be proved by the hot fountains and fiery phenomena which must have been so familiar to a native of Sicily. Curiously enough he imagined fire to possess a solidifying power, and therefore attributed to it the solidity of the earth and the hardness of the rocks. No doubt he had observed some effects of fire in 'metamorphic' formations in his own vicinity.

He had also a conception of the gradual development on the earth of higher and higher forms of life, the first being rude and imperfect, and a 'struggle for existence' ensuing in which the monstrous and the deficient gradually were eliminated—the "two-faced, the double-breasted, the oxen-shaped with human prows, or human-shaped with head of ox, or hemaphrodite," and so forth. Love and Strife worked out their ends upon these varied forms; some procreated and reproduced after their image, others were incapable of reproduction from mere monstrosity or weakness, and disappeared. Something other than mere chance thus governed the development of things; there was a law, a reason, a *Logos* governing the process. This law or reason he perhaps fancifully illustrated by attributing the different characters of flesh and sinew and bone to the different numerical proportions, in which they severally contain the different elements.

On this Aristotle, keen-scented critic as he was, has a question, or series of questions, to ask as to the relation between this Logos, or principle of orderly combination, and Love as the ruling force in all unions of things. "Is Love," he asks, "a cause of mixtures of any sort, or only of such sorts as Logos dictates? And whether then is Love identical with this Logos, or are they separate and distinct; and if so, what settles their separate functions?" Questions which Empedocles did not answer, and perhaps would not have tried to answer had he heard them.

The soul or life-principle in man Empedocles regarded as an ordered composite of all the elements or principles of the life in nature, and in this kinship of the elements in man and the elements in nature he found a rationale of our powers of perception. "By the earth," said he, "we have perception of earth; by water we have perception of water; of the divine aether, by aether; of destructive fire, by fire; of love, by love; of strife, by strife." He therefore, as Aristotle observes, drew no radical distinction between sense-apprehension and thought. He located the faculty of apprehension more specifically in the blood, conceiving that in it the combination of the elements was most complete. And the variety of apprehensive gift in different persons he attributed to the greater or lesser perfectness of this blood mixture in them individually. Those that were dull and stupid had a relative deficiency of the lighter and more invisible elements; those that were quick and impulsive had a relatively larger proportion of these. Again, specific faculties depended on local perfection of mixture in certain organs; orators having this perfectness in their tongues, cunning craftsmen possessing it in their hands, and so on. And the degrees of capacity of sensation, which he found in various animals, or even plants, he explained in similar fashion.

The process of sensation he conceived to be conditioned by an actual emission from the bodies perceived of elements or images of themselves which found access to our apprehension through channels congruous to their nature. But ordering, criticizing, organizing these various apprehensions was the Mind or *Nous*, which he conceived to be of divine nature, to be indeed an expression or emanation of the Divine. And here has been preserved a strangely interesting passage, in which he incorporates and develops in characteristic fashion the doctrine of transmigration of souls: "There is a decree of Necessity, a law given of old from the gods, eternal, sealed with mighty oaths, that when any heavenly creature (daemon) of those that are endowed with length of days, shall in waywardness of heart defile his hands with sin of deed or speech, he shall wander for thrice ten thousand seasons far from the dwellings of the blest, taking upon him in length of time all manner of mortal forms, traversing in turn the many toilsome paths of existence. Him the aetherial wrath hurries onward to the deep, and the deep spews him forth on to the threshold of earth, and unworn earth casts him up to the fires of the sun, and again the aether hurls him into the eddies. One receives him, and then another, but detested is he of them all. Of such am I also one, an exile and a wanderer from God, a slave to strife and its madness."

Thus to his mighty conception the life of all creation, and not of man only, was a great expiation, an eternal round of punishment for sin; and in the unending flux of life each creature rose or fell in the scale of existence according to the deeds of good or ill done in each successive life; rising sometimes to the state of men, or among men to the high functions of physicians and prophets and kings, or among beasts to the dignity of the lion, or among trees to the beauty of the laurel; or, on the contrary, sinking through sin to lowest forms of bestial or vegetable life. Till at the last they who through obedience and right-doing have expiated their wrong, are endowed by the blessed gods with endless honor, to dwell for ever with them and share their banquets, untouched any more with human care and sorrow and pain.

The slaying of any living creature, therefore, Empedocles, like Pythagoras, abhorred, for all were kin. All foul acts were forms of worse than suicide; life should be a long act of worship, of expiation, of purification. And in the dim past he pictured a vision of a golden age, in which men worshipped not many gods, but Love only, and not with sacrifices of blood, but with pious images, and cunningly odorous incense, and offerings of fragrant myrrh. With abstinence also, and above all with that noblest abstinence, the abstinence from vice and wrong.

CHAPTER VIII

THE ATOMISTS (*concluded*)

The laughing philosopher—Atoms and void—No god and no truth

III. LEUCIPPUS AND DEMOCRITUS.—Leucippus is variously called a native of Elea, of Abdera, of Melos, of Miletus. He was a pupil of Zeno the Eleatic. Democritus was a native of Abdera. They seem to have been almost contemporary with Socrates. The two are associated as thorough-going teachers of the 'Atomic Philosophy,' but Democritus, 'the laughing philosopher,' as he was popularly called in later times, in distinction from Heraclitus, 'the weeping philosopher,' was much the more famous. He lived to a great age. He himself refers to his travels and studies thus: "Above all the men of my time I travelled farthest, and extended my inquiries to places the most distant. I visited the most varied climates and countries, heard the largest number of learned men, nor has any one surpassed me in the gathering together of writings and their interpretation, no, not even the most learned of the Egyptians, with whom I spent five years." We are also informed that, through desire of learning, he visited Babylon and Chaldaea, to visit the astrologers and the priests.

Democritus was not less prolific as a writer than he was voracious as a student, and in him first the division of philosophy into certain great sections, such as physical, mathematical, ethical, was clearly drawn. We are, however, mainly concerned with his teaching in its more strictly philosophical aspects. His main doctrine was professedly antithetical to that of the Eleatics, who, it will be remembered, worked out on abstract lines a theory of one indivisible, eternal, immovable Being. Democritus, on the contrary, declared for two co-equal elements, the Full and the Empty, or Being and Nonentity. The latter, he maintained, was as real as the former. As we should put it, Body is unthinkable except by reference to space which that body does not occupy, as well as to space which it does occupy; and conversely Space is unthinkable except by reference to body actually or potentially filling or defining it.

What Democritus hoped to get by this double or correlative system was a means of accounting for or conceiving of *change* in nature. The difficulty with the Eleatics was, as we have seen, how to understand whence or why the transition from that which absolutely is, to this strange, at least apparent, system of eternal flux and transformation. Democritus hoped to get over this difficulty by starting as fully with that which *is not*, in other words, with that which *wants* change in order to have any recognizable being at all, as with that which *is*, and which therefore might be conceived as seeking and requiring only to be what it is.

Having got his principle of stability and his principle of change on an equal footing, Democritus next laid it down that all the differences visible in things were differences either of shape, of arrangement, or of position; practically, that is, he considered that what seem, to us to be qualitative differences in things, *e.g.* hot or cold, sweet or sour, green or yellow, are only resulting impressions from different shapes, or different arrangements, or different modes of presentation, among the atoms of which things are composed.

Coming now to that which *is*, Democritus, as against the Eleatics, maintained that this was not a unity, someone immovable, unchangeable existence, but an innumerable number of atoms, invisible by reason of their smallness, which career through empty space (that which *is not*), and by their union bring objects into being, by their separation bring these to destruction. The action of these atoms on each other depended on the manner in which they were brought into contact; but in any case the unity of any object was only an apparent unity, it being really constituted of a multitude of interlaced and mutually related particles, and all growth or increase of the object being conditioned by the introduction into the structure of additional atoms from without.

For the motions of the atoms he had no anterior cause to offer, other than necessity or fate. They existed, and necessarily and always had existed, in a state of whirl; and for that which always had been he maintained that no preceding cause could legitimately or reasonably be demanded.

Nothing, then, could come out of nothing; all the visible structure of the universe had its origin in the movements of the atoms that constituted it, and conditioned its infinite changes. The atoms, by a useful but perhaps too convenient metaphor, he called the *seeds* of all things. They were infinite in number, though not infinite in the number, of their shapes. Many atoms were similar to each other, and this similarity formed a basis of union among them, a warp, so to speak, or solid foundation across which the woof of dissimilar atoms played to constitute the differences of things.

Out of this idea of an eternal eddy or whirl Democritus developed a cosmogony. The lighter atoms he imagined flew to the outmost rim of the eddy, there constituting the heavenly fires and the heavenly aether. The heavier atoms gathered at the centre, forming successively air and water and the solid earth. Not that there was only one such system or world, but rather multitudes of them, all varying one from the other; some without sun or moon, others with greater luminaries than those of our system, others with a greater number. All, however, had necessarily a centre; all as systems were necessarily spherical.

As regards the atoms he conceived that when they differed in weight this must be in respect of a difference in their essential size. In this he was no doubt combating the notion that the atoms say of lead or gold were in their substance, taking equal quantities, of greater weight than atoms of water or air. The difference of weight in objects depended on the proportion which the atoms in them bore to the amount of empty space which was interlaced with them. On the other hand, a piece of iron was lighter yet harder than a piece of lead of equal size, because of the special way in which the atoms in it were linked together. There were fewer atoms in it, but they were, in consequence of their structure and arrangement, more tightly strung.

In all this Democritus was with great resolution working out what we may call a strictly mechanical theory of the universe. Even the soul or life-principle in living creatures was simply a structure of the finest and roundest (and therefore most nimble) atoms, with which he compared the extremely attenuated dust particles visible in their never-ending dance in a beam of light passed into a darkened room. This structure of exceeding tenuity and nimbleness was the source of the motion characteristic of living creatures, and provided that elastic counteracting force to the inward-pressing nimble air, whereby were produced the phenomena of respiration. Every object, in fact, whether living or not, kept its form and distinctive existence by its possession in degree of a kind of soul or spirit of resistance in its structure, adequate to counteract the pressure of external forces upon its particles.

Sensation and perception were forms in which these external forces acted upon the more nimble and lively existences, more particularly on living creatures. For everybody was continually sending forth emanations or images resembling itself sufficiently in form and structure to affect perceptive bodies with an apprehension of that form and structure. These images travelled by a process of successive transmission, similar to that by which wave-motions are propagated in water. They were, in other words, not movements of the *particles* of the objects, which latter must otherwise in time grow less and fade away, but a modification in the arrangement of the particles immediately next the object, which modification reproduced itself in the next following, and so on right through the medium to the perceptive body.

These images tended by extension in all directions to reach vast dimensions at times, and to influence the minds of men in sleep and on other occasions in strange ways. Hence men imagined gods, and attributed those mighty phenomena of nature—earthquakes, tempests, lightning and thunder, and dire eclipses of sun and moon, to the vaguely visible powers which they imagined they saw. There was indeed a soul or spirit of the universe, as there was a soul or spirit of every individual thing that constituted it. But this was only a finer system of atoms after all. All else is convention or dream; the only realities are Atoms and Emptiness, Matter and Space.

Of absolute verity through the senses we know nothing; our perceptions are only conventional interpretations of we know not what. For to other living creatures these same sensations have other meanings than they have to us, and even the same person is not always affected alike by the same thing; which then is the true of two differing perceptions we cannot say. And therefore either there is no such thing as truth, or, at all events, we know through the senses nothing of it. The only genuine knowledge is that which transcends appearances, and reasons out what is, irrespective of appearances,—in other words, the only genuine knowledge is that of the (atomic) philosopher. And his knowledge is the result of the happy mixture of his atoms whereby all is in equal balance, neither too hot nor too cold. Such a man seeing in the mind's eye the whole universe a tissue of whirling and interlacing atoms, with no real mystery or terror before or after, will live a life of cheerful fearlessness, undisturbed by terrors of a world to come or of powers unseen. His happiness is not in feastings or in gold, but in a mind at peace. And three human perfections he will seek to attain: to reason rightly, to speak graciously, to do his duty.

CHAPTER IX

THE SOPHISTS

Anarchic philosophy—Success not truth—Man the measure—All opinions true—Reductio ad absurdum

A certain analogy may perhaps be discerned between the progression of philosophic thought in Greece as we have traced it, and the political development which had its course in almost every Greek state during the same period. The Ionic philosophy may be regarded as corresponding with the *kingly* era in Greek politics. Philosophy sits upon the heights and utters its authoritative dicta for the resolution of the seeming contradictions of things. One principle is master, but the testimony of the senses is not denied; a harmony of thought and sensation is sought in the interpretation of appearances by the light of a ruling idea. In Pythagoras and his order we have an *aristocratic* organization of philosophy. Its truths are for the few, the best men are the teachers, equal as initiated partakers in the mysteries, supreme over all outside their society. A reasoned and reasonable order and method are symbolized by their theory of Number; their philosophy is political, their politics oligarchic. In the Eleatic school we have a succession of personal attempts to construct a *domination* in the theory of Nature; some ideal conception is attempted to be so elevated above the data of sensation as to override them altogether, and the general result we are now to see throughout the philosophic world, as it was seen also throughout the world of politics, in a total collapse of the principle of forced authority, and a development, of successively nearer approaches to anarchic individualism and doubt. The notion of an ultimately true and real, whatever form it might assume in various theorists' hands, being in its essence apart from and even antagonistic to the perceptions of sense, was at last definitely cast aside as a delusion; what remained were the individual perceptions, admittedly separate, unreasoned, unrelated; Reason was dethroned, Chaos was king. In other words, what *seemed* to any individual sentient being at any moment to be, that for him was, and nothing else was. The distinction between the real and the apparent was definitely attempted to be abolished, not as hitherto by rejecting the sensually apparent in favor of the rationally conceived real, but by the denial of any such real altogether.

The individualistic revolution in philosophy not only, however, had analogies with the similar revolution contemporaneously going on in Greek politics, it was greatly facilitated by it. Each, in short, acted and reacted on the other. Just as the skeptical philosophy of the Encyclopaedists in France promoted the Revolution, and the Revolution in its turn developed and confirmed the philosophic skepticism, so also the collapse of contending philosophies in Greece promoted the collapse of contending systems of political authority, and the collapse of political authority facilitated the growth of that individualism in thought with which the name of the Sophists is associated.

Cicero (*Brut.* 12) definitely connects the rise of these teachers with the expulsion of the tyrants and the establishment of democratic republics in Sicily. From 466 to 406 B.C. Syracuse was democratically governed, and a 'free career to talents,' as in revolutionary France, so also in revolutionary Greece, began to be promoted by the elaboration of a system of persuasive argument. Devices of method called 'commonplaces' were constructed, whereby, irrespective of the truth or falsehood of the subject-matter, a favorable vote in the public assemblies, a successful verdict in the public courts, might more readily be procured. Thus by skill of verbal rhetoric, the worse might be made to appear the better reason; and philosophy, so far as it continued its functions, became a search, not for the real amidst the confusions of the seeming and unreal, but a search for the seeming and the plausible, to the detriment, or at least to the ignoring, of any reality at all.

The end of philosophy then was no longer universal truth, but individual success; and consistently enough, the philosopher himself professed the individualism of his own point of view, by teaching only those who were prepared to pay him for his teaching. All over Greece, with the growth of democracy, this philosophy of persuasion became popular; but it was to Athens, under Pericles at this time the centre of all that was most vivid and splendid in Greek life and thought, that the chief teachers of the new philosophy flocked from every part of the Greek world.

The first great leader of the Sophists was *Protagoras.* He, it is said, was the first to teach for pay; he also was the first to adopt the name of Sophist. In the word Sophist there was indeed latent the idea which subsequently attached to it, but as first used it seems to have implied this only, that *skill* was the object of the teaching rather than *truth*; the new teachers professed themselves 'practical men,' not mere theorists.

The Greek word, in short, meant an able cultivated man in any branch of the arts; and the development of practical capacity was doubtless what Protagoras intended to indicate as the purpose of his teaching, when he called himself a Sophist. But the ability he really undertook to cultivate was ability to *persuade*, for Greece at this time was nothing if not political; and persuasive oratory was the one road to political success. And as Athens was the great centre of Greek politics, as well as of Greek intellect, to Athens Protagoras came as a teacher.

He was born at Abdera, in Thrace (birthplace also of Democritus), in 480 B.C., began to teach at Athens about 451 B.C., and soon acquired great influence with Pericles, the distinguished leader of the Athenian democracy at this time. It is even alleged that when in 445 the Athenians were preparing to establish a colony at

Thurii in Italy, Protagoras was requested to draw up a code of laws for the new state, and personally to superintend its execution.

After spending some time in Italy he returned to Athens, and taught there with great success for a number of years. Afterwards he taught for some time in Sicily, and died at the age of seventy, after about forty years of professional activity. He does not seem to have contented himself with the merely practical task of teaching rhetoric, but in a work which he, perhaps ironically, entitled *Truth*, he enunciated the principles on which he based his teaching. Those principles were summed up in the sentence, "Man (by which he meant *each* man) is the measure of all things, whether of their existence when they do exist, or of their non-existence when they do not." In the development of this doctrine Protagoras starts from a somewhat similar analysis of things to that of Heraclitus and others. Everything is in continual flux, and the apparently real objects in nature are the mere temporary and illusory result of the in themselves invisible movements and minglings of the elements of which they are composed; and not only is it a delusion to attempt to give a factitious reality to the things which appear, it is equally a delusion to attempt to separate the (supposed) thing perceived from the perception itself. A thing is only as and when it is perceived. And a third delusion is to attempt to separate a supposed perceiving mind from the perception; all three exist only in and through the momentary perception; the supposed reality behind this, whether external in the object or internal in the mind, is a mere imagination. Thus the Heraclitean flux in Nature was extended to Mind also; only the sensation exists, and that only at the moment of its occurrence; this alone is truth, this alone is reality; all else is delusion.

It followed from this that as a man felt a thing to be, so for him it veritably was. Thus abstract truth or falsity could not be; the same statements could be indifferently true or false—to different individuals at the same time, to the same individual at different times. It followed that all appearances were equally true: what seemed to be to any man, that was alone the true for him. The relation of such a doctrine as this to politics and to morals is not far to seek. Every man's opinion was as good as another's; if by persuasion you succeeded in altering a man's opinion, you had not deceived the man, his new opinion was as true (to him) as the old one. Persuasiveness, therefore, was the only wisdom. Thus if a man is ill what he eats and drinks seems bitter to him, and it is so; when he is well it seems the opposite, and is so. He is not a wiser man in the second state than in the first, but the second state is pleasanter. If then you can persuade him that what he thinks bitter is really sweet, you have done him good. This is what the physician tries to do by his drugs; this is what the Sophist tries to do by his words. Virtue then is teachable in so far as it is possible to persuade a boy or a man by rhetoric that that course of conduct which pleases others is a pleasant course for him. But if any one happens not to be persuaded of this, and continues to prefer his own particular course of conduct, this *is* for him the good course. You cannot blame him; you cannot say he is wrong. If you punish him you simply endeavor to supply the dose of unpleasantness which may be needed to put the balance in his case on the same side as it already occupies in the case of other people.

It may be worthwhile to anticipate a little, and insert here in summary the refutation of this position put into the mouth of Socrates by Plato in the

Theaetetus: "But I ought not to conceal from you that there is a serious objection which may be urged against this doctrine of Protagoras. For there are states, such as madness and dreaming, in which perception is false; and half our life is spent in dreaming; and who can say that at this instant we are not dreaming? Even the fancies of madmen are real at the time. But if knowledge is perception, how can we distinguish between the true and the false in such cases? . . . Shall I tell you what amazes me in your friend Protagoras? 'What may that be?' I like his doctrine that what appears is; but I wonder that he did not begin his great work on truth with a declaration that a pig, or a dog-faced baboon, or any other monster which has sensation, is a measure of all things; then while we were reverencing him as a god he might have produced a magnificent effect by expounding to us that he was no wiser than a tadpole. For if truth is only sensation, and one man's discernment is as good as another's, and every man is his own judge, and everything that he judges is right and true, then what need of Protagoras to be our instructor at a high figure; and why should we be less knowing than he is, or have to go to him, if every man is the measure of all things?" . . . Socrates now resumes the argument. As he is very desirous of doing justice to Protagoras, he insists on citing his own words: 'What appears to each man is to him.' "And how," asks Socrates, "are these words reconcilable with the fact that all mankind are agreed in thinking themselves wiser than others in some respects, and inferior to them in others? In the hour of danger they are ready to fall down and worship anyone who is their superior in wisdom as if he were a god. And the world is full of men who are asking to be taught and willing to be ruled, and of other men who are willing to rule and teach them. All which implies that men do judge of one another's impressions, and think some wise and others foolish. How will Protagoras answer this argument? For he cannot say that no one deems another ignorant or mistaken. If you form a judgment, thousands and tens of thousands are ready to maintain the opposite. The multitude may not and do not agree in Protagoras' own thesis, 'that man is the measure of all things,' and then who is to decide? Upon hip own showing must not his 'truth' depend on the number of suffrages, and be more or less true in proportion as he has more or fewer of them? And [the majority being against him] he will be bound to acknowledge that they speak truly who deny him to speak truly, which is a famous jest. And if he admits that they speak truly who deny him to speak truly, he must admit that he himself does not speak truly. But his opponents will refuse to admit this as regards themselves, and he must admit that they are right in their refusal. The conclusion is, that all mankind, including Protagoras himself, will deny that he speaks truly; and his truth will be true neither to himself nor to anybody else" (Jowett, *Plato*, iv. pp. 239 *sqq.*)

The refutation seems tolerably complete, but a good deal had to happen before Greece was ready to accept or Plato to offer such a refutation.

CHAPTER X

THE SOPHISTS (*concluded*)

Nothing knowable—The solitude of scepticism—The lawlessness of scepticism— The good in scepticism

Gorgias was perhaps even more eminent a Sophist than Protagoras. He was a native of Leontini in Sicily, and came to Athens in the year 427 B.C. on a public embassy from his native city. The splendid reputation for political and rhetorical ability, which preceded him to Athens, he fully justified both by his public appearances before the Athenian assembly, and by the success of his private instructions to the crowds of wealthy young men who resorted to him. He dressed in magnificent style, and affected a lofty and poetical manner of speech, which offended the more critical, but which pleased the crowd.

He also, like Protagoras, published a treatise in which he expounded his fundamental principles, and like Protagoras, he preceded it with a striking if somewhat ironical title, and an apophthegm in which he summarized his doctrine. The title of his work was *Of the Non-Existent*, that is, *Of Nature*, and his dictum, "Nothing exists, or if anything exists, it cannot be apprehended by man, and even if it could be apprehended, the man who apprehended it could not expound or explain it to his neighbor." In support of this strange doctrine, Gorgias adopted the quibbling method of argument which had been applied with some success to dialectical purposes by Zeno, Melissus, and others.

His chief argument to prove the first position laid down by him depended on a double and ambiguous use of the word *is*; "That which is not, *is* the non-existent: the word *is* must, therefore, be applicable to it as truly as when we say That which is, *is*; therefore, being is predicable of that which is not." So conversely he proved not-being to be predicable of that which is. And in like manner he made away with any possible assertions as to the finite or infinite, the eternal or created, nature of that which is. Logic could supply him with alternative arguments from whatever point he started, such as would seem to land the question in absurdity. Hence his first position was (he claimed) established, that 'Nothing is.'

To prove the second, that even if anything is, it cannot be known to man, he argued thus: "If what a man thinks is not identical with what is, plainly what is cannot be thought. And that what a man thinks is not identical with what is can be shown from the fact that thinking does not affect the facts. You may imagine a man flying, or a chariot coursing over the deep, but you do not find these things to occur because you imagine them. Again, if we assume that what we think is identical with what is, then it must be impossible to think of what is not. But this is absurd; for we can think of such admittedly imaginary beings as Scylla and Chimaera, and multitudes of others. There is therefore no necessary relation between our thoughts and any realities; we may believe, but we cannot prove, which (if any) of our conceptions have relation to an external fact and which have not."

Nor thirdly, supposing any man had obtained an apprehension of what is real, could he possibly communicate it to anyone else. If a man saw anything, he could not possibly by verbal description make clear what it is he sees to a man who has never seen. And so if a man has not himself the apprehension of reality, mere words from another cannot possibly give him any idea of it. He may imagine he has the same idea as the speaker, but where is he going to get the common test by which to establish the identity?

Without attempting to follow Gorgias further, we can see plainly enough the object and purport of the whole doctrine. Its main result is to *isolate*. It isolates each man from his fellows; he cannot tell what they know or think, they cannot reach any common ground with him. It isolates him from nature; he cannot tell what nature is, he cannot tell whether he knows anything of nature or reality at all. It isolates him from himself; he cannot tell for certain what relation exists (if any) between what he imagines he perceives at any moment and any remembered or imagined previous experiences; he cannot be sure that there ever were any such experiences, or what that self was (if anything) which had them, or whether there was or is any self perceiving anything.

Let us imagine the moral effect on the minds of the ablest youth of Greece of such an absolute collapse of belief. The philosophic skepticism did not deprive them of their appetites or passions; it did not in the least alter their estimate of the prizes of success, or the desirability of wealth and power. All it did was to shatter the invisible social bonds of reverence and honor and truth and justice, which in greater or less degree act as a restraining force upon the purely selfish appetites of men. Not only belief in divine government disappeared, but belief in any government external or internal; justice became a cheating device to deprive a man of what was ready to his grasp; good-faith was stupidity when it was not a more subtle form of deceit; morality was at best a mere convention which a man might cancel if he pleased; the one reality was the appetite of the moment, the one thing needful its gratification; society, therefore, was universal war, only with subtler weapons.

Of course Protagoras and Gorgias were only notable types of a whole horde of able men who in various ways, and with probably less clear notions than these men of the drift or philosophic significance of their activity, helped all over Greece in the promulgation of this new gospel of self-interest. Many Sophists no doubt troubled themselves very little with philosophical questions; they were 'agnostics,' know-nothings; all they professed to do was to teach some practical skill of a verbal or rhetorical character. They had nothing to do with the nature or value of ideals; they did not profess to say whether any end or aim was in itself good or bad, but given an end or aim, they were prepared to help those who hired them to acquire a skill which would be useful towards attaining it.

But whether a philosophy or ultimate theory of life be expressly stated or realized by a nation or an individual, or be simply ignored by them, there always is some such philosophy or theory underlying their action, and that philosophy or theory tends to work itself out to its logical issue in action, whether men openly profess it or no. And the theory of negation of law in nature or in man which underlay the sophistic practice had its logical and necessary effect on the social structure throughout Greece, in a loosening of the bonds of religion, of family reverence and affection, of patriotism, of law, of honor. Thucydides in a well-known passage (iii. 82) thus describes the prevalent condition of thought in his own time, which was distinctively that of the sophistic teaching: "The common meaning of words was turned about at men's pleasure; the most reckless bravo was deemed the most desirable friend; a man of prudence and moderation was styled a coward; a man who listened to reason was a good-for-nothing simpleton. People were trusted exactly in proportion to their violence and unscrupulousness, and no one was so popular as the successful conspirator, except perhaps one who had been clever enough to outwit him at his own trade, but anyone who honestly attempted to remove the causes of such treacheries was considered a traitor to his party. As for oaths, no one imagined they were to be kept a moment longer than occasion required; it was, in fact, an added pleasure to destroy your enemy if you had managed to catch him through his trusting to your word."

These are the words not of Plato, who is supposed often enough to allow his imagination to carry him beyond his facts about the Sophists as about others, nor are they the words of a satiric poet such as Aristophanes. They are the words of the most sober and philosophic of Greek historians, and they illustrate very strikingly the tendency, nay, the absolute necessity, whereby the theories of philosophers in the closet extend themselves into the market-place and the home, and find an ultimate realization of themselves for good or for evil in the 'business and bosoms' of the common crowd.

It is not to be said that the individualistic and iconoclastic movement which the Sophists represented was wholly bad, or wholly unnecessary, any more (to again quote a modern instance) than that the French Revolution was. There was much, no doubt, in the traditional religion and morality of Greece at that time which represented obsolete and antiquated conditions, when every city lived apart from its neighbors with its own narrow interests and local cults and ceremonials. Greece was ceasing to be an unconnected crowd of little separate communities; unconsciously it was preparing itself for a larger destiny, that of conqueror and civilizer of East and West. This skepticism, utterly untenable and unworkable on the lines extravagantly laid down by its leading teachers, represented the birth of new conditions of thought and action adapted to the new conditions of things. On the surface, and accepted literally, it seemed to deny the possibility of knowledge; it threatened to destroy humanity and civilization. But its strength lay latent in an implied denial only of what was merely traditional; it denied the finality of purely Greek preconceptions; it was laying the foundations of a broader humanity. It represented the claim of a new generation to have no dogma or assumption thrust on it by mere force, physical or moral. "*I* too am a man," it said; "*I* have rights; *my* reason must be convinced." This is the fundamental thought at the root of most revolutions and reformations and revivals, and the thought is therefore a necessary and a just one.

Unfortunately it seems to be an inevitable condition of human affairs that nothing new, however necessary or good can come into being out of the old, without much sorrow and many a birth-pang. The extravagant, the impetuous, the narrow-minded on both sides seize on their points of difference, raise them into battle-cries, and make what might be a peaceful regeneration a horrid battlefield of contending hates. The Christ when He comes brings not peace into the world, but a sword. And men of evil passions and selfish ambitions are quick on both sides to make the struggle of old and new ideals a handle for their own indulgence or their own advancement; the Pharisees and the Judases between them make the Advent in some of its aspects a sorry spectacle.

A reconciler was wanted who should wed what was true in the new doctrine of individualism with what was valuable in the old doctrine of universal and necessary truth; who should be able to say, "Yes, I acknowledge that your individual view of things must be reckoned with, and mine, and everybody else's; and for that very reason do I argue for a universal and necessary truth, because the very truth for you as an individual is just this universal." The union and identification of the Individual and Universal,—this paradox of philosophy is the doctrine of Socrates.

CHAPTER XI

SOCRATES

The crisis of philosophy—Philosophic midwifery—The wisest of men—The gadfly of Athens—Justice, beauty, utility—Virtue is knowledge

The sophistic teaching having forced philosophy to descend into the practical interests and personal affairs of men, it followed that any further step in philosophy, any reaction against the Sophists, could only begin from the moral point of view. Philosophy, as an analysis of the data of perception or of nature, had issued in a social and moral chaos. Only by brooding on the moral chaos could the spirit of truth evoke a new order; only out of the moral darkness could a new intellectual light be made to shine. The social and personal anarchy seemed to be a *reductio ad absurdum* of the philosophy of nature; if ever the philosophy of nature was to be recovered it must be through a revision of the theory of morals. If it could be proved that the doctrine of individualism, of isolation, which the analysis of a Protagoras or a Gorgias had reached, was not only *unlivable* but unthinkable,—carried the seeds of its own destruction, theoretical as well as practical, within itself,—then the analysis of *perception*, from which this moral individualism issued, might itself be called to submit to revision, and a stable point of support in the moral world might thus become a centre of stability for the intellectual and the physical also.

By a perfectly logical process, therefore, the crisis of philosophy produced in Greece through the moral and social chaos of the sophistic teaching had two issues, or perhaps we may call it one issue, carried out on the one side with a less, on the other side with a greater completeness. The less complete reaction from sophistic teaching attempted only such reconstruction of the moral point of view as should recover a law or principle of general and universally cogent character, whereon might be built anew a *moral* order without attempting to extend the inquiry as to a universal principle into the regions of abstract truth or into physics. The more complete and logical reaction, starting, indeed, from a universal principle in morals, undertook a logical reconstruction on the recovered universal basis all along the line of what was knowable.

To Socrates it was given to recover the lost point of stability in the world of morals, and by a system of attack, invented by himself, to deal in such a manner with the anarchists about him as to prepare the way for his successors, when the time was ripe for a more extended exposition of the new point of view. Those who in succession to him worked out a more limited theory of law, mainly or exclusively in the world of morals, only were called the *Incomplete Socratics*. Those who undertook to work it out through the whole field of the knowable, the *Complete Socratics*, were the two giants of philosophy, Plato and Aristotle.

Greek philosophy then marks with the life of Socrates a parting of the ways in two senses: *first*, inasmuch as with him came the reaction from a physical or theoretical philosophy, having its issue in a moral chaos; and *second*, inasmuch as from him the two great streams of later philosophy issued—the one a philosophy of law or universals in *action*, the other a philosophy of law or universals in *thought* and *nature* as well.

Socrates, son of Sophroniscus a sculptor and Phaenarete a midwife, was born at Athens in or about the year 469 B.C. His parents were probably poor, for Socrates is represented as having been too poor to pay the fees required for instruction by the Sophists of his time. But in whatever way acquired or assimilated, it is certain that there was little of the prevalent culture in cultivated Athens with which Socrates had not ultimately a working acquaintance.

Among a people distinguished generally for their handsome features and noble proportions, Socrates was a notable exception. His face was squat and round, his eyes protruding, his lips thick; he was clumsy and uncouth in appearance, careless of dress, a thorough 'Bohemian,' as we should call him. He was, however, gifted with an uncommon bodily vigor, was indifferent to heat and cold, by temperament moderate in food and drink, yet capable on occasion of drinking most people 'under the table.' He was of an imperturbable humor, not to be excited either by danger or by ridicule. His vein of sarcasm was keen and trenchant, his natural shrewdness astonishing, all the more astonishing because crossed with a strange vein of mysticism and a curious self-forgetfulness. As he grew up he felt the visitation of a mysterious internal voice, to which or to his own internal communings he would sometimes be observed to listen in abstracted stillness for hours. The voice within him was felt as a restraining force, limiting his action in various ways, but leaving him free to wander about among his fellows, to watch their doings and interpret their thoughts, to question unweariedly his fellows of every class, high and low, rich and poor, concerning righteousness and justice and goodness and purity and truth. He did not enter on his philosophic work with some grand general principle ready-made, to which he was prepared to fit the facts by hook or by crook. Rather he compared himself to his mother, the midwife; he sought to help others to express themselves; he had nothing to tell them, he wanted them to tell him. This was the irony of Socrates, the eternal *questioning*, which in time came to mean in people's minds what the word does now. For it was hard, and grew every year harder, to convince people that so subtle a questioner was as ignorant as he professed to be; or that the man who could touch so keenly the weak point of all other men's answers, had no answer to the problems of life himself.

In striking contrast, then, to the method of all previous philosophies, Socrates busied himself to begin with, not with some general intellectual *principle*, but with a multitude of different *people*, with their notions especially on moral ideas, with the meaning or no-meaning which they attached to particular words,—in short, with the individual, the particular, the concrete, the every-day. He did not at all deny that he had a purpose in all this. On the contrary, he openly professed that he was in search of the lost universal, the lost *law* of men's thoughts and actions. He was convinced that life was not the chaos that the Sophists made out; that nobody really believed it to be a chaos; that, on the contrary, everybody had a meaning and purport in his every word and act, which could be made intelligible to himself and others, if you could only get people to think out clearly what they really meant. Philosophy had met her destruction in the busy haunts of men; there where had been the bane, Socrates' firm faith sought ever and everywhere the antidote.

This simple enough yet profound and far-reaching practice of Socrates was theorized in later times as a logical method, known to us as *Induction*, or the discovery of universal laws or principles out of an accumulation of particular facts. And thus Aristotle, with his technical and systematizing intellect, attributes two main innovations in philosophy to Socrates; the *Inductive* process of reasoning, and the establishing of *General Ideas* or Definitions upon or through this process. This, true enough as indicating what was latent in the Socratic method, and what was subsequently actually developed out of it by Aristotle himself, is nevertheless probably an anachronism if one seeks to represent it as consciously present in Socrates' mind. Socrates adopted the method unconsciously, just because he wanted to get at the people about him, and through them at what they thought. He was the pioneer of Induction rather than its inventor; he created, so to speak, the raw material for a theory of induction and definition; he knew and cared nothing about such theories himself.

A story which may or may not be true in fact is put in Socrates' mouth by Plato, as to the cause which first started him on his "search for definitions." One of his friends, he tells us, named Chaerephon, went to the oracle of Apollo at Delphi, and asked whether there was anybody wiser than Socrates. The answer was given that there was none wiser. This answer was reported to Socrates, who was much astonished, his own impression being that he had no wisdom or knowledge at all. So with a view to prove the oracle wrong he went in succession to various people of eminence and reputation in the various walks of life,—statesmen and poets and handicraftsmen and others,—in the expectation that they would show, on being questioned, such a knowledge of the principles on which their work was based as would prove their superior wisdom. But to his astonishment he found one after another of these men wanting in any apprehension of principles at all. They seemed to work by a kind of haphazard or 'rule of thumb,' and indeed felt annoyed that anything more should be expected of them. From which at the last Socrates came to the conclusion that perhaps the oracle was right in this sense at least, that, if he himself knew nothing more than his fellows, he was at least conscious of his own ignorance, whereas they were not.

Whether this tale may not itself be a specimen of Socrates' irony we cannot tell, but at all events it illustrates from another point of view the real meaning of Socrates' life. He, at least, was not content to rest in haphazard and rule of thumb; he was determined to go on till he found out what was the law or principle of men's acts and words. The ignorance of others as to any such law or principle in their own case did not convince him that there was no such law or principle; only it was there (he thought) working unconsciously, and therefore in a way defenselessly. And so he compares himself at times to a gadfly, whose function it is to sting and irritate people out of their easy indifference, and force them to ask themselves what were really driving at. Or again, he compares himself to the torpedo-fish, because he tried to give people a shock whenever they attempted to satisfy him with shallow and unreal explanations of their thoughts and actions.

The disinterested self-sacrificing nobility of Socrates' life, thus devoted to awakening them that sleep out of their moral torpor; the enmities that his keen and trenchant questionings of quacks and pretenders of every kind induced; the devotion of some of his friends, the unhappy falling away of others; the calumnies of interested enemies, the satires of poets; and lastly, the story of the final attack by an ungrateful people on their one great teacher, of his unjust condemnation and heroic death—all this we must pass over here. The story is in outline, at least, a familiar one, and it is one of the noblest in history. What is more to the purpose for us is to ascertain how far his search for definitions was successful; how far he was able to

Take arms against a sea of troubles

And by opposing end them;

how far, in short, he was able to evolve a law, a universal principle, out of the confused babel of common life and thought and speech, strong enough and wide enough on which to build a new order for this world, a new hope for the world beyond.

We have said that Socrates made the individual and the concrete the field of his search. And not only did he look to individuals for light, he looked to each individual specifically in that aspect of his character and faculty which was most particular to himself. That is to say, if he met a carpenter, it was on his carpentering that he questioned him; if a sculptor, on his practice as a sculptor; if a statesman, on his statesmanship. In short, he did not want general vague theories on subjects of which his interlocutors could not be supposed to have any special experience or knowledge; he interrogated each on the subject which he knew best.

And what struck him, in contrast to the confusion and uncertainty and isolation of the sophistic teaching 'in the air,' was that when you get a man to talk on his own trade, which he *knows*, as is proved by the actual work he produces, you find invariably two things—*first*, that the skill is the man's *individual* possession no doubt, the result of inborn capacity and continuous training and practice; but *second*, that just in proportion to that individual skill is the man's conviction that his skill has reference to a *law* higher than himself, outside himself. If the man whom Socrates interviewed was a skilful statesman, he would tell you he sought to produce obedience to *law* or right among the citizens; if he was a skilful sculptor, he produced *beautiful* things; if he was a skilful handicraftsman, he produced *useful* things. Justice, beauty, utility; these three words in different ways illustrated the existence of something always realizing itself no doubt in individuals and their works, but nevertheless exercising a governing influence upon these to such a degree that this ideal something might be conceived as *prior* to the individual or his work; or secondly, as *inherent* in them and giving value to them; or thirdly, as coming in at the end as the *perfection* or completion of them. This law or ideal then had a threefold aspect in its own nature, being conceivable as Justice, as Beauty, as Utility; it had a threefold aspect in relation to the works produced in accordance with it, as the cause *producing*, the cause *inhering*, the cause completing or *perfecting*.

We may therefore conceive Socrates as arguing thus: "You clever Sophists, when we let you take us into the region of abstract talk, have a knack of so playing with words that in the end we don't seem to know anything for certain, especially on such subjects as we have hitherto thought the most important, such as God and right and truth and justice and purity. We seem to be perfectly defenseless against you; and what is more, any smart youth, whose opinion on any practical matter no one would think of taking, can very soon pick up the trick from you, and bewilder plain people really far wiser than himself by his clever argumentation; all going to prove that there is nothing certain, nothing real, nothing binding; nothing but opinions and conventions and conscious or unconscious humbug in the universe.

"But when I go and have a quiet talk with any man who really is a known master of some craft or skill, about that craft or skill, I find no doubt whatever existing in his mind about there being a law, a something absolutely real and beautiful and true in connection with it. He, on the contrary, lives with no other purpose or hope or desire but as far as he can to realize in what he works at something of this real and beautiful and true, which was before him, will be after him, is the only valuable thing in him, but yet which honors him with the function of, in his day and generation, expressing it before the eyes of men."

"Have we not here a key to the great secret? If each man, in respect of that which he knows best because he lives by it and for it, knows with intimate knowledge and certainty that there at least there is a Law working, not himself, but higher and greater than he,—have we not here a hint of the truth for the universe as a whole; that there also and in all its operations, great as well as small, there must be a Law, a great Idea or Ideal working, which was before all things, works in and gives value to all things, will be the consummation of all things? Is not this what we mean by the Divine?"

Thus Socrates, despising not the meaner things of life, but bending from the airy speculations of the proud to the realities which true labor showed him, laid his ear, so to speak, close to the breast of nature, and caught there the sound of her very heart-beats.

"Virtue is knowledge," thus he formulated his new vision of things. Knowledge, yes; but *real* knowledge; not mere head-knowledge or lip-knowledge, but the knowledge of the skilled man, the man who by obedience and teachableness and self-restraint has come to a knowledge evidencing itself in *works* expressive of the law that is in him, as he is in it. *Virtue is knowledge*; on the one hand, therefore, not something in the air, unreal, intangible; but something in me, in you, in each man, something which you cannot handle except as individual and in individuals; on the other hand, something more than individual or capricious or uncertain,— something which is absolute, over-ruling, eternal.

Virtue is knowledge. And so if a man is virtuous, he is realizing what is best and truest in himself, he is fulfilling also what is best and truest without himself. He is free, for only the truth makes free; he is obedient to law, but it is at once a law eternally valid, and a law which he dictates to himself. And therefore virtue is teachable, inasmuch as the law in the teacher, perfected in him, is also the law in the taught, latent in him, by both individually possessed, but possessed by both in virtue of its being greater than both, of its being something more than individual.

Virtue is knowledge. And therefore the law of virtuous growth is expressed in the maxim engraved on the Delphic temple, 'Know thyself.' Know thyself, that is, realize thyself; by obedience and self-control come to your full stature; be in fact what you are in possibility; satisfy yourself, in the only way in which true self-satisfaction is possible, by realizing in yourself the law which constitutes your real being.

Virtue is knowledge. And therefore all the manifold relations of life,—the home, the market, the city, the state; all the multiform activities of life,—labor and speech and art and literature and law; all the sentiments of life,—friendship and love and reverence and courage and hope,—all these are parts of a knowable whole; they are expressions of law; they are Reason realizing itself through individuals, and in the same process realizing them.

CHAPTER XII

SOCRATES (*concluded*)

The dialectic method—Instruction through humiliation—Justice and utility—Righteousness transcending rule

It must not be imagined that anywhere in the recorded conversations of Socrates can we find thus in so many words expounded his fundamental doctrine. Socrates was not an expositor but a questioner; he disclaimed the position of a teacher, he refused to admit that any were his pupils or disciples. But his questioning had two sides, each in its way leading people on to an apprehension of the ideal in existence. The first side may be called the negative or destructive, the second, the positive or constructive. In the first, whose object was to break down all formalism, all mere regard for rules or traditions or unreasoned maxims, his method had considerable resemblance to that of the Sophists; like them he descended not infrequently to what looked very like quibbling and word-play. As Aristotle observes, the dialectic method differed from that of the Sophists not so much in its form, as in the purpose for which it was employed. The end of the Sophists was to confuse, the end of Socrates was through confusion to reach a more real, because a more reasoned certainty; the Sophists sought to leave the impression that there was no such thing as truth; he wished to lead people to the conviction that there was a far deeper truth than they were as yet possessed of.

A specimen of his manner of conversation preserved for us by Xenophon (*Memor.* IV. ii.) will make the difference clearer. Euthydemus was a young man who had shown great industry in forming a collection of wise sayings from poets and others, and who prided himself on his superior wisdom because of his knowledge of these. Socrates skillfully manages to get the ear of this young man by commending him for his collection, and asks him what he expects his learning to help him to become? A physician? No, Euthydemus answers. An architect? No. And so in like manner with other practical skills,—the geometrician's, astronomer's, professional reciter's. None of these he discovers is what Euthydemus aims at. He hopes to become a great politician and statesman. Then of course he hopes to be a just man himself? Euthydemus flatters himself he is that already. "But," says Socrates, "there must be certain acts which are the proper products of justice, as of other functions or skills?"—"No doubt."—"Then of course you can tell us what those acts or products are?"—"Of course I can, and the products of injustice as well."—"Very good; then suppose we write down in two opposite columns what acts are products of justice and what of injustice."—"I agree," says Euthydemus.—"Well now, what of falsehood? In which column shall we put it?"—"Why, of course in the unjust column."—"And cheating?"—"In the same column."—"And stealing?"—"In it too."—"And enslaving?"—"Yes."—"Not one of these can go to the just column?"—"Why, that would be an unheard-of thing."

"Well but," says Socrates, "suppose a general has to deal with some enemy of his country that has done it great wrong; if he conquer and enslave this enemy, is that wrong?"—"Certainly not."—"If he carries off the enemy's goods or cheats him in his strategy, what about these acts?"—"Oh, of course they are quite right. But I thought you were talking about deceiving or ill-treating friends."—"Then in some cases we shall have to put these very same acts in both columns?"—"I suppose so."

"Well, now, suppose we confine ourselves to friends. Imagine a general with an army under him discouraged and disorganized. Suppose he tells them that reserves are coming up, and by cheating them into this belief he saves them from their discouragement, and enables them to win a victory. What about this cheating of one's friends?"—"Why, I suppose we shall have to put this too on the just side."—"Or suppose a lad needs medicine, but refuses to take it, and his father cheats him into the belief that it is something nice, and getting him to take it, saves his life; what about that cheat?"—"That will have to go to the just side too."—"Or suppose you find a friend in a desperate frenzy, and steal his sword from him, for fear he should kill himself; what do you say to that theft?"—"That will have to go there too."—"But I thought you said there must be no cheating of friends?"—"Well, I must take it all back, if you please."—"Very good. But now there is another point I should like to ask you. Whether do you think the man more unjust who is a voluntary violator of justice, or he who is an involuntary violator of it?"—"Upon my word, Socrates, I no longer have any confidence in my answers. For the whole thing has turned out to be exactly the contrary of what I previously imagined. However, suppose I say that the voluntary deceiver is the more unjust."—"Do you consider that justice is a matter of knowledge just as much (say) as writing?"—"Yes, I do."—"Well now, which do you consider the better skilled as a writer, the man who makes a mistake in writing or in reading what is written, because he chooses to do so, or the man who does so because he can't help it?"—"Oh, the first; because he can put it right whenever he likes."—"Very well, if a man in the same way breaks the rule of right, knowing what he is doing, while another breaks the same rule because he can't help it, which by analogy must be the better versed in justice?"—"The first, I suppose."—"And the man who is better versed in justice must be the juster man?"—"Apparently so; but really, Socrates, I don't know where I am. I have been flattering myself that I was in possession of a philosophy which could make a good and able man of me. But how great, think you, must now be my disappointment, when I find myself unable to answer the simplest question on the subject?"

Many other questions are put to him, tending to probe his self-knowledge, and in the end he is brought to the conclusion that perhaps he had better hold his tongue, for it seems he knows nothing at all. And so he went away deeply despondent, despising himself as an absolute dolt. "Now many," adds Xenophon, "when brought into this condition by Socrates, never came near him again. But Euthydemus concluded that his only hope of ever being worth anything was in seeing as much of Socrates as he could, and so he never quitted his side as long as he had a chance, but tried to follow his mode of living. And Socrates, when he perceived this to be his temper, no longer tormented him, but sought with all simplicity and clearness to show him what he deemed it best for him to do and think."

Was this cross-examination mere 'tormenting' with a purpose, or can we discover underlying it any hint of what Socrates deemed to be the truth about justice?

Let us note that throughout he is in search of a *definition*, but that as soon as any attempt is made to define or classify any particular type of action as just or unjust, *special circumstances* are suggested which overturn the classification. Let us note further that while the immediate result is apparently only to confuse, the remoter but more permanent result is to raise a suspicion of any hard and fast definitions, and to suggest that there is something deeper in life than language is adequate to express, a 'law in the members,' a living principle for good, which transcends forms and maxims, and which alone gives real value to acts. Note further the suggestion that this living principle has a character analogous to the knowledge or skill of an accomplished artificer; it has relation on the one hand to law, as a principle binding on the individual, it has relation on the other hand to *utility*, as expressing itself, not in words, but in acts beneficial to those concerned. Hence the Socratic formula, Justice is equivalent to the *Lawful* on the one hand, to the *Useful* on the other.

Socrates had thus solved by anticipation the apparently never-ending controversy about morality. Is it a matter imposed by God upon the heart and conscience of each individual? Is it dictated by the general sense of the community? Is it the product of Utility? The Socratic answer would be that it is all three, and that all three mean ultimately the same thing. What God prescribes is what man when he is truly man desires; and what God prescribes and man desires is that which is good and useful for man. It is not a matter for verbal definition but for vital realization; the true morality is that which *works*; the ideally desirable, is ultimately the only possible, course of action, for all violations of it are ultimately suicidal.

Note finally the suggestion that the man who *knows* (in Socrates' sense of knowledge) what is right, shows only more fully his righteousness when he voluntarily sins; it is the 'unwilling sinner' who is the wrongdoer. When we consider this strange doctrine in relation to the instances given,—the general with his army, the father with his son, the prudent friend with his friend in desperate straits,—we see that what is meant is that 'sin' in the real sense is not to be measured or defined by conformity or otherwise to some formal standard, at least in the case of those who *know*, that is, in the case of men who have realised goodness in its true nature in their characters and lives. As St. Paul expressed it (Rom. xiii. 10), "Love is the fulfilling of the law." Or again (Gal. v. 23), after enumerating the 'fruits of the spirit'—love, joy, peace, longsuffering, gentleness, goodness, faith, meekness, temperance—he adds, "Against such there is no law."

In the domain of life, not less than in that of the arts, the highest activity does not always or necessarily take the form of conformity to rule. There are critical moments when rules fail, when, in fact, obedience to rule would mean disobedience to that higher law, of which rules and formulae are at best only an adumbration. The originality of the great musician or painter consists in just such transcendence of accepted formulae; this is why he invariably encounters opposition and obloquy from the learned conventional pedants of his time. And in the domain of morals the martyrs, reformers, prophets are in like manner 'willing sinners.' They are denounced, persecuted, crucified; for are they not disturbers of society; do they not unsettle young men; do they not come, as Christ came, not to bring peace into the world, but a sword? And thus it is that the willing sinners of one generation are the martyrs and heroes of the next. Through their life and death a richer meaning has been given to the law of beauty or of rectitude, only, alas! in its turn to be translated into new conventions, new formulae, which shall in due time require new martyrs to transcend them. And thus, on the other hand, the perfectly honest sticklers for the old and common-place, unwilling sinners all unconscious of their sin, are fated to bear in history the brand of men who have persecuted the righteous without cause. To each, according to the strange sad law of life, time brings its revenges.

CHAPTER XIII

THE INCOMPLETE SOCRATICS

A philosopher at ease—The sensual sty—Citizens of the world—The tub of Diogenes—A philosophy of abstracts

I. ARISTIPPUS AND THE CYRENAICS.—Aristippus was a native of Cyrene, a Greek colony on the north coast of Africa. He is said to have come to Athens because of his desire to hear Socrates; but from the notices of him which we find in Xenophon's memoirs he appears to have been from the first a somewhat intractable follower, dissenting especially from the poverty and self-denial of the master's mode of life. He in course of time founded a school of his own, called the Cyrenaic from his own place of birth, and from the fact that many subsequent leaders of the school also belonged to Cyrene. Among his notable disciples were his daughter Arete, her son named Aristippus after his grandfather, Ptolemaeus the Aethiopian, Antipater of Cyrene, and a long succession of others.

Aristippus was a man of considerable subtlety of mind, a ready speaker, clever in adapting himself to persons and circumstances. On one occasion, being asked what benefit he considered philosophy had conferred upon him, he answered, "The capacity of associating with every one without embarrassment." Philosophy, in fact, was to Aristippus a method of social culture, a means of making the best of life as he found it. As Horace observes of him (*Epp.* i. 17. 23)—

Omnis Aristippum decuit color et status et res
Tentantem majora, fere praesentibus aequum.

"Every aspect and manner of life and fortune fitted Aristippus; he aimed at what was greater, yet kept an even, mind whatever his present condition."

As we have already said, this school was *incompletely* Socratic, inasmuch as philosophy was not an end in itself, knowledge whether of oneself or of other matters had no intrinsic interest for them; philosophy was only a means towards pleasurable living, enabling them so to analyse and classify the several experiences of life as to render a theory of satisfactory existence possible. With them first came into prominence a phrase which held a large place in all subsequent Greek philosophy, the *End* of existence, by which was meant that which summed up the good in existence, that which made life worth living, that which was good and desirable in and for itself, and not merely as a means to something else. What then according to the Cyrenaics was the End of life? Their answer was that life had at each moment its own End, in the pleasure of that moment. The past was gone, the future not yet with us; remembrance of the one, fear or hope of the other, might contribute to affect the purity of the present pleasure, but such as it was the present pleasure was a thing apart, complete in and for itself. Nor was its perfection qualified by any question of the means by which it was procured; the moment's pleasure was pleasurable, whatever men might say as to the manner of its procuring. This pleasure was a tranquil activity of the being, like the gently heaving sea, midway between violent motion which was pain, and absolute calm which was insensibility. As a state of activity it was something positive, not a mere release from pain, not a simple filling up of a vacuum. Nothing was in its essential nature either just or noble or base; custom and convention pronounced them one or other. The wise man made the best he could of his conditions; valuing mental activity and friendship and wealth and bodily exercise, and avoiding envy and excessive indulgence of passion and superstition, not because the first were in themselves good or the second evil, but because they were respectively helpers or hinderers of pleasure. He is the master and possessor of pleasure not who abstains from it, but who uses it and keeps his self-command in the using. Moderate indulgence—this is wisdom.

The one criterion, whether of good or of truth, is the feeling of the moment for the man who feels it; all question of causes of feelings is delusive. We can say with truth and certainty, I have the sensation of white or the sensation of sweet. But that there is a white or a sweet thing which is the cause of the sensation, that we cannot say for certain. A man may very well have the sensation white or sweet from something which has no such quality, as men in delusion or madness have impressions that are true and real inasmuch as they have them, although other people do not admit their reality. There is, therefore, no criterion of truth as between man and man; we may employ the same words, but each has his own impressions and his own individual experiences.

One can easily understand this as the doctrine of such a man as Aristippus, the easy-going man of the world, the courtier and the wit, the favorite of the tyrant Dionysius; it fits in well enough with a life of genial self-indulgence; it always reappears whenever a man has reconciled himself 'to roll with pleasure in a sensual sty.' But life is not always, nor for most persons at any time, a thing of ease and soft enchantments, and the Cyrenaic philosophy must remain for the general work-a-day world a stale exotic. 'Every man for himself and the devil take the hindmost,' is a maxim which comes as a rule only to the lips of the worldly successful, while they think themselves strong enough to stand alone. But this solitude of selfishness neither works nor lasts; every man at some time becomes 'the hindmost,' if not before, at least in the hour of death for him or his; at that hour he is hardly disposed, for himself or those he loves, to repeat his maxim.

II. ANTISTHENES AND THE CYNICS.—Aristippus, in his praises of pleasure as the one good for man, remarks that there were some who refused pleasure "from perversity of mind," taking pleasure, so to speak, in the denial of pleasure. The school of the Cynics made this perverse mood, as Aristippus deemed it, the maxim of their philosophy. As the Cyrenaic school was the school of the rich, the courtly, the self-indulgent, so the Cynic was the school of the poor, the exiles, the ascetics. Each was an extreme expression of a phase of Greek life and thought, though there was this point of union between them, that *liberty* of a kind was sought by both. The Cyrenaics claimed liberty to please themselves in the choice of their enjoyments; the Cynics sought liberty through denial of enjoyments. Both, moreover, were cosmopolitan; they mark the decay of the Greek patriotism, which was essentially civic, and the rise of the wider but less intense conception of humanity. Aristippus, in a conversation with Socrates (Xenoph. *Memor*. II. i.) on the qualifications of those who are fitted to be magistrates, disclaims all desire to hold such a position himself. "There is," he says, "to my thinking, a middle way, neither of rule nor of slavery, but of freedom, which leads most surely to true happiness. So to avoid all the evils of partisanship and faction I nowhere take upon me the position of a citizen, but in every city remain a sojourner and a stranger." And in like manner Antisthenes the Cynic, being asked how a man should approach politics, answered, "He will approach it as he will fire, not too near, lest he be burnt; not too far away, lest he starve of cold." And Diogenes, being asked of what city he was, answered, "I am a citizen of the world." The Cynic ideal, in fact, was summed up in these four words—wisdom, independence, free speech, liberty.

Antisthenes, founder of the school, was a native of Athens, but being of mixed blood (his mother was a Thracian) he was not recognized as an Athenian citizen. He was a student first under Gorgias, and acquired from him a considerable elegance of literary style; subsequently he became a devoted hearer of Socrates, and became prominent among his followers for an asceticism surpassing his master's. One day, we are told, he showed a great rent in the thread-bare cloak which was his only garment, whereupon Socrates slily remarked, "I can see through your cloak your love of glory." He carried a leathern scrip and a staff, and the 'scrip and staff' became distinctive marks of his school. The name Cynic, derived from the Greek word for a dog, is variously accounted for, some attributing it to the 'doglike' habits of the school, others to their love of 'barking' criticism, others to the fact that a certain gymnasium in the outskirts of Athens, called Cynosarges, sacred to Hercules the patron-divinity of men in the political position of Antisthenes, was a favorite resort of his. He was a voluminous, some thought a too voluminous, expounder of his tenets. Like the other Incomplete Socratics, his teaching was mainly on ethical questions.

His chief pupil and successor was the famous Diogenes, a native of Sinope, a Greek colony on the Euxine Sea. He even bettered the instructions of his master in the matter of extreme frugality of living, claiming that he was a true follower of Hercules in preferring independence to every other good. The tale of his living in a cask or tub is well known. His theory was that the peculiar privilege of the gods consisted in their need of nothing; men approached nearest the life of the gods in needing as little as possible.

Many other sayings of one or other teacher are quoted, all tending to the same conclusion. For example, "I had rather be mad than enjoying myself!" "Follow the pleasures that come after pains, not those which bring pains in their train." "There are pains that are useless, there are pains that are natural: the wise choose the latter, and thus find happiness even through pain. For the very contempt of pleasure comes with practice to be the highest pleasure." "When I wish a treat," says Antisthenes, "I do not go and buy it at great cost in the marketplace; I find my storehouse of pleasures in the soul."

The life of the wise man, therefore, was a training of mind and body to despise pleasure and attain independence. In this way virtue was teachable, and could be so acquired as to become an inseparable possession. The man who had thus attained to wisdom, not of words, but of deeds, was, as it were, in an impregnable fortress that could neither crumble into ruin nor be lost by treachery. And so Antisthenes, being asked what was the most essential point of learning, answered, "To unlearn what is evil." That is to say, to the Cynic conception, men were born with a root of evil in them in the love of pleasure; the path of wisdom was a weaning of soul and body by practice from the allurements of pleasure, until both were so perfectly accustomed to its denial as to find an unalloyed pleasure in the very act of refusing it. In this way virtue became absolutely sufficient for happiness, and so far was it from being necessary to have wealth or the admiration of men in addition, that the true kingly life was "to do well, and be ill spoken of." All else but virtue was a matter of indifference.

The cosmopolitan temper of these men led them to hold of small account the forms and prejudices of ordinary society: they despised the rites of marriage; they thought no flesh unclean. They believed in no multifarious theology; there was but one divinity—the power that ruled all nature, the one absolutely self-centered independent being, whose manner of existence they sought to imitate. Nor had they any sympathy with the subtleties of verbal distinction cultivated by some of the Socratics, as by other philosophers or Sophists of their time. Definitions and abstractions and classifications led to no good. A man was a man; what was good was good; to say that a man was good did not establish the existence of some abstract class of goods. As Antisthenes once said to Plato, "A horse I see, but 'horseness' I do not see." What the exact point of this criticism was we may reserve for the present.

III. EUCLIDES THE MEGARIC.—Euclides, a native of Megara on the Corinthian isthmus, was a devoted hearer of Socrates, making his way to hear him, sometimes even at the 'risk of his life, in defiance of a decree of his native city forbidding intercourse with Athens. When Plato and other Athenian followers of Socrates thought well to quit Athens for a time after Socrates' execution, they were kindly entertained by Euclides at Megara.

The exact character of the development which the Socratic teaching received from Euclides and his school is a matter of considerable doubt. The allusions to the tenets of the school in Plato and others are only fragmentary. We gather, however, from them that Euclides was wholly antithetical to the personal turn given to philosophy, both by the Cyrenaics and the Cynics. He revived and developed with much dialectical subtlety the metaphysical system of Parmenides and the Eleatics, maintaining that there is but one absolute existence, and that sense and sense-perceptions as against this are nothing. This one absolute existence was alone absolutely good, and the good for man could only be found in such an absorption of himself in this one absolute good through reason and contemplation, as would bring his spirit into perfectness of union with it. Such absorption raised a man above the troubles and pains of life, and thus, in insensibility to these through reason, man attained his highest good.

The school is perhaps interesting only in so far as it marks the continued survival of the abstract dialectic method of earlier philosophy. As such it had a very definite influence, sometimes through agreement, sometimes by controversy, on the systems of Plato and Aristotle now to be dealt with.

CHAPTER XIV

PLATO

Student and wanderer—The Dialogues—Immortal longings—Art is love—Knowledge through remembrance—Platonic love

This great master, the Shakespeare of Greek philosophy, as one may call him, for his fertility, his variety, his humor, his imagination, his poetic grace, was born at Athens in the year 429 B.C. He was of noble family, numbering among his ancestors no less a man than the great lawgiver Solon, and tracing back his descent even further to the legendary Codrus, last king of Athens. At a very early age he seems to have begun to study the philosophers, Heraclitus more particularly, and before he was twenty he had written a tragedy. About that time, however, he met Socrates; and at once giving up all thought of poetic fame he burnt his poem, and devoted himself to the hearing of Socrates. For ten years he was his constant companion. When Socrates met his death in 399, Plato and other followers of the master fled at first to Megara, as already mentioned; he then entered on a period of extended travel, first to Cyrene and Egypt, thence to Italy and Sicily. In Italy he devoted himself specially to a study of the doctrine of Pythagoras. It is said that at Syracuse he offended the tyrant Dionysius the elder by his freedom of speech, and was delivered up to the Spartans, who were then at war with Athens. Ultimately he was ransomed, and found his way back to Athens, but he is said to have paid a second visit to Sicily when the younger Dionysius became tyrant. He seems to have entertained the hope that he might so influence this young man as to be able to realize through him the dream of his life, a government in accordance with the dictates of philosophy. His dream, however, was disappointed of fruition, and he returned to Athens, there in the 'groves of Academus' a mythic hero of Athens, to spend the rest of his days in converse with his followers, and there at the ripe age of eighty-one he died. From the scene of his labors his philosophy has ever since been known as the Academic philosophy. Unlike Socrates, he was not content to leave only a memory of himself and his conversations. He was unwearied in the redaction and correction of his written dialogues, altering them here and there both in expression and in structure. It is impossible, therefore, to be absolutely certain as to the historical order of composition or publication among his numerous dialogues, but a certain approximate order may be fixed.

We may take first a certain number of comparatively short dialogues, which are strongly Socratic in the following respects: *first*, they each seek a definition of some particular virtue or quality; *second*, each suggests some relation between it and knowledge; *third*, each leaves the answer somewhat open, treating the matter suggestively rather than dogmatically. These dialogues are *Charmides*, which treats of Temperance (*mens sana in corpore sano*); *Lysis*, which treats of Friendship; *Laches*, Of Courage; *Ion*, Of Poetic Inspiration; *Meno*, Of the teachableness of Virtue; *Euthyphro*, Of Piety.

The last of these may be regarded as marking a transition to a second series, which are concerned with the trial and death of Socrates. The *Euthyphro* opens with an allusion by Socrates to his approaching trial, and in the *Apology* we have a Platonic version of Socrates' speech in his own defense; in *Crito* we have the story of his noble self-abnegation and civic obedience after his condemnation; in *Phaedo* we have his last conversation with his friends on the subject of Immortality, and the story of his death.

Another series of the dialogues may be formed of those, more or less satirical, in which the ideas and methods of the Sophists are criticized: *Protagoras*, in which Socrates suggests that all virtues are essentially one; *Euthydemus*, in which the assumption and 'airs' of some of the Sophists are made fun of; *Cratylus*, Of the sophistic use of words; *Gorgias*, Of the True and the False, the truly Good and the truly Evil; *Hippias*, Of Voluntary and Involuntary Sin; *Alcibiades*, Of Self-Knowledge; *Menexenus*, a (possibly ironical) set oration after the manner of the Sophists, in praise of Athens.

The whole of this third series are characterized by humor, dramatic interest, variety of personal type among the speakers, keenness rather than depth of philosophic insight. There are many suggestions of profounder thoughts, afterwards worked out more fully; but on the whole these dialogues rather stimulate thought than satisfy it; the great poet-thinker is still playing with his tools.

A higher stage is reached in the *Symposium*, which deals at once humorously and profoundly with the subject of Love, human and divine, and its relations to Art and Philosophy, the whole consummated in a speech related by Socrates as having been spoken to him by Diotima, a wise woman of Mantineia. From this speech an extract as translated by Professor Jowett may be quoted here. It marks the transition point from the merely playful and critical to the relatively serious and dogmatic stage in the mind of Plato:—

"Marvel not," she said, "if you believe that love is of the immortal, as we have already several times acknowledged; for here again, and on the same principle too, the mortal nature is seeking as far as is possible to be everlasting and immortal: and this is only to be attained by generation, because generation always leaves behind a new existence in the place of the old. Nay even in the life of the same individual there is succession and not absolute unity: a man is called the same, and yet in the short interval which elapses between youth and age, and in which every animal is said to have life and identity, he is undergoing a perpetual process of loss and reparation—hair, flesh, bones, blood, and the whole body are always changing. Which is true not only of the body, but also of the soul, whose habits, tempers, opinions, desires, pleasures, pains, fears, never remain the same in any one of us, but are always coming and going; and equally true of knowledge, which is still more surprising—for not only do the sciences in general come and go, so that in respect of them we are never the same; but each of them individually experiences a like change. For what is implied in the word 'recollection,' but the departure of knowledge, which is ever being forgotten and is renewed and preserved by recollection, and appears to be the same although in reality new, according to that law of succession by which all mortal things are preserved, not absolutely the same, but by substitution, the old worn-out mortality leaving another new and similar existence behind—unlike the divine, which is always the same and not another? And in this way, Socrates, the mortal body, or mortal anything, partakes of immortality; but the immortal in another way. Marvel not then at the love which all men have of their offspring; for that universal love and interest is for the sake of immortality."

I was astonished at her words, and said: "Is this really true, O thou wise Diotima?" And she answered with all the authority of a sophist: "Of that, Socrates, you may be assured;—think only of the ambition of men, and you will wonder at the senselessness of their ways, unless you consider how they are stirred by the love of an immortality of fame. They are ready to run risks greater far than they would have run for their children, and to spend money and undergo any sort of toil, and even to die for the sake of leaving behind them a name which shall be eternal. Do you imagine that Alcestis would have died to save Admetus, or Achilles to avenge Patroclus, or your own Codrus in order to preserve the kingdom for his sons, if they had not imagined that the memory of their virtues, which is still retained among us, would be immortal? Nay," she said, "I am persuaded that all men do all things, and the better they are the more they do them, in hope of the glorious fame of immortal virtue; for they desire the immortal.

"They whose bodies only are creative, betake themselves to women and beget children—this is the character of their love; their offspring, as they hope, will preserve their memory and give them the blessedness and immortality which they desire in the future. But creative souls—for there certainly are men who are more creative in their souls than in their bodies—conceive that which is proper for the soul to conceive or retain. And what are these conceptions?—wisdom and virtue in general. And such creators are poets and all artists who are deserving of the name inventor. But the greatest and fairest sort of wisdom by far is that which is concerned with the ordering of states and families, and which is called temperance and justice. And he who in youth has the seed of these implanted in him and is himself inspired, when he comes to maturity desires to beget and generate. He wanders about seeking beauty that he may beget offspring—for in deformity he will beget nothing—and naturally embraces the beautiful rather than the deformed body; above all when he finds a fair and noble and well-nurtured soul, he embraces the two in one person, and to such an one he is full of speech about virtue and the nature and pursuits of a good man; and he tries to educate him; and at the touch of the beautiful which is ever present to his memory, even when absent, he brings forth that which he had conceived long before, and in company with him tends that which he brings forth; and they are married by a far nearer tie and have a closer friendship than those who beget mortal children, for the children who are their common offspring are fairer and more immortal. Who, when he thinks of Homer and Hesiod and other great poets, would not rather have their children than ordinary human ones? Who would not emulate them in the creation of children such as theirs, which have preserved their memory and given them everlasting glory? Or who would not have such children as Lycurgus left behind him to be the saviors, not only of Lacedaemon, but of Hellas, as one may say? There is Solon, too, who is the revered father of Athenian laws; and many others there are in many other places, both among Hellenes and barbarians. All of them have given to the world many noble works, and have been the parents of virtue of every kind, and many temples have been raised in their honor for the sake of their children; which were never raised in honor of any one, for the sake of his mortal children.

"These are the lesser mysteries of love, into which even you, Socrates, may enter; to the greater and more hidden ones which are the crown of these, and to which, if you pursue them in a right spirit, they will lead, I know not whether you will be able to attain. But I will do my utmost to inform you, and do you follow if you can. For he who would proceed aright in this matter should begin in youth to visit beautiful forms; and first, if he be guided by his instructor aright, to love one such form only—out of that he should create fair thoughts; and soon he will of himself perceive that the beauty of one form is akin to the beauty of another; and then if beauty of form in general is his pursuit, how foolish would he be not to recognize that the beauty in every form is one and the same! And when he perceives this he will abate his violent love of the one, which he will despise and deem a small thing, and will become a lover of all beautiful forms; in the next stage he will consider that the beauty of the mind is more honorable than the beauty of the outward form. So that if a virtuous soul have but a little comeliness, he will be content to love and tend him, and will search out and bring to the birth thoughts which may improve the young, until he is compelled to contemplate and see the beauty of institutions and laws, and to understand that the beauty of them all is of one family, and that personal beauty is a trifle; and after laws and institutions he will go on to the sciences, that he may see their beauty, being not like a servant in love with the beauty of one youth or man or institution, himself a slave mean and narrow-minded, but drawing towards and contemplating the vast sea of beauty, he will create many fair and noble thoughts and notions in boundless love of wisdom; until on that shore he grows and waxes strong, and at last the vision is revealed to him of a single science, which is the science of beauty everywhere. To this I will proceed; please to give me your very best attention.

"He who has been instructed thus far in the things of love, and who has learned to see the beautiful in due order and succession, when he comes toward the end will suddenly perceive a nature of wondrous beauty (and this, Socrates, is the final cause of all our former toils)—a nature which in the first place is everlasting, not growing and decaying, or waxing and waning, in the next place not fair in one point of view and foul in another, or at one time or in one relation or at one place fair, at another time or in another relation or at another place foul, as if fair to some and foul to others, or in the likeness of a face or hands or any other part of the bodily frame, or in any form of speech or knowledge, or existing in any other being; as for example, in an animal, or in heaven, or in earth, or in any other place, but beauty only, absolute, separate, simple, and everlasting, which without diminution and without increase, or any change, is imparted to the ever-growing and perishing beauties of all other things. He who under the influence of true love rising upward from these begins to see that beauty, is not far from the end. And the true order of going or being led by another to the things of love, is to use the beauties of earth as steps along which he mounts upwards for the sake of that other beauty, going from one to two, and from two to all fair forms, and from fair forms to fair practices, and from fair practices to fair notions, until from fair notions he arrives at the notion of absolute beauty, and at last knows what the essence of beauty is. This, my dear Socrates," said the stranger of Mantineia, "is that life above all others which a man should live, in the contemplation of beauty absolute; a beauty which if you once beheld, you would see not to be after the measure of gold, and garments, and fair boys and youths, whose presence now entrances you; and you and many a one would be content to live seeing only and conversing with them without meat or drink, if that were possible—you only want to be with them and to look at them. But what if man had eyes to see the true beauty—the divine beauty, I mean, pure and clear and unalloyed, not clogged with the pollutions of mortality, and all the colors and vanities of human life—thither looking, and holding converse with the true beauty divine and simple? Do you not see that in that communion only, beholding beauty with the eye of the mind, he will be enabled to bring forth, not images of beauty, but realities (for he has hold not of an image but of a reality), and bringing forth and nourishing true virtue to become the friend of God and be immortal, if mortal man may. Would that be an ignoble life?" (Jowett, *Plato*, vol. ii. p. 58).

Closely connected in subject with the *Symposium* is the *Phaedrus*. As Professor Jowett observes: "The two dialogues together contain the whole philosophy of Plato on the nature of love, which in *The Republic* and in the later writings of Plato is only introduced playfully or as a figure of speech. But in the *Phaedrus* and *Symposium* love and philosophy join hands, and one is an aspect of the other. The spiritual and emotional is elevated into the ideal, to which in the *Symposium* mankind are described as looking forward, and which in the *Phaedrus*, as well as in the *Phaedo*, they are seeking to recover from a former state of existence."

We are here introduced to one of the most famous conceptions of Plato, that of *Reminiscence*, or Recollection, based upon a theory of the prior existence of the soul. In the *Meno*, already alluded to, Socrates is representing as eliciting from one of Meno's slaves correct answers to questions involving a knowledge or apprehension of certain axioms of the science of mathematics, which, as Socrates learns, the slave had never been taught. Socrates argues that since he was never taught these axioms, and yet actually knows them, he must have known them before his birth, and concludes from this to the immortality of the soul. In the *Phaedo* this same argument is worked out more fully. As we grow up we discover in the exercise of our senses that things are equal in certain respects, unequal in many others; or again, we appropriate to things or acts the qualities, for example, of beauty, goodness, justice, holiness. At the same time we recognize that these are *ideals*, to which in actual experience we never find more than an approximation, for we never discover in any really existing thing or act *absolute* equality, or justice, or goodness. In other words, any act of judgment on our part of actual experiences consists in a measuring of these experiences by standards which we give or apply to them, and which no number of experiences can give to us because they do not possess or exemplify them. We did not consciously possess these notions, or ideals, or *ideas*, as he prefers to call them, at birth; they come into consciousness in connection with or in consequence of the action of the senses; but since the senses could not give these ideas, the process of knowledge must be a process of *Recollection*. Socrates carries the argument a step further. "Then may we not say," he continues, "that if, as we are always repeating, there is an absolute beauty and goodness and other similar ideas or essences, and to this standard, which is now discovered to have existed in our former state, we refer all our sensations, and with this compare them—assuming these ideas to have a prior existence, then our souls must have had a prior existence, but if not, not? There is the same proof that these ideas must have existed before we were born, as that our souls existed before we were born; and if not the ideas, then not the souls."

In the *Phaedrus* this conception of a former existence is embodied in one of the *Myths* in which Plato's imaginative powers are seen at their highest. In it the soul is compared to a charioteer driving two winged steeds, one mortal, the other immortal; the one ever tending towards the earth, the other seeking ever to soar into the sky, where it may behold those blessed visions of loveliness and wisdom and goodness, which are the true nurture of the soul. When the chariots of the gods go forth in mighty and glorious procession, the soul would fain ride forth in their train; but alas! the mortal steed is ever hampering the immortal, and dragging it down.

If the soul yields to this influence and descends to earth, there she takes human form, but in higher or lower degree, according to the measure of her vision of the truth. She may become a philosopher, a king, a trader, an athlete, a prophet, a poet, a husbandman, a sophist, a tyrant. But whatever her lot, according to her manner of life in it, may she rise, or sink still further, even to a beast or plant.

Only those souls take the form of humanity that have had *some* vision of eternal truth. And this vision they retain in a measure, even when clogged in mortal clay. And so the soul of man is ever striving and fluttering after something beyond; and specially is she stirred to aspiration by the sight of bodily loveliness. Then above all comes the test of good and evil in the soul. The nature that has been corrupted would fain rush to brutal joys; but the purer nature looks with reverence and wonder at this beauty, for it is an adumbration of the celestial joys which he still remembers vaguely from the heavenly vision. And thus pure and holy love becomes an opening back to heaven; it is a source of happiness unalloyed on earth; it guides the lovers on upward wings back to the heaven whence they came.

CHAPTER XV

PLATO (continued)

The Republic—Denizens of the cave—The Timaeus—A dream of creation

And now we pass to the central and crowning work of Plato, *The Republic*, or *Of Justice*—the longest with one exception, and certainly the greatest of all his works. It combines the humor and irony, the vivid characterization and lively dialogue of his earlier works, with the larger and more serious view, the more constructive and statesmanlike aims of his later life. The dialogue opens very beautifully. There has been a festal procession at the Piraeus, the harbor of Athens, and Socrates with a companion is wending his way homeward, when he is recalled by other companions, who induce him to visit the house of an aged friend of his, Cephalus, whom he does not visit too often. Him he finds seated in his court, crowned, as the custom was, for the celebration of a family sacrifice, and beholds beaming on his face the peace of a life well spent and reconciled. They talk of the happiness that comes in old age to those who have done good and not evil, and who are not too severely tried in the matter of worldly cares. Life to this good old man seems a very simple matter; duty to God, duty to one's neighbors, each according to what is prescribed and orderly; this is all, and this is sufficient.

Then comes in the questioning Socrates, with his doubts and difficulties as to what is one's duty in special circumstances; and the discussion is taken up, not by the good old man, "who goes away to the sacrifice," but by his son, who can quote the authorities; and by Thrasymachus, the Sophist, who will have nothing to do with authority, but maintains that *interest* is the only real meaning of justice, and that Might is Right. Socrates, by analogy of the arts, shows that Might absolutely without tincture of justice is mere weakness, and that there is honor even among thieves. Yet the exhibition of the 'law working in the members' seems to have its weak side so long as we look to individual men, in whom there are many conflicting influences, and many personal chances and difficulties, which obscure the relation between just action and happiness.

Socrates therefore will have justice 'writ large' in the community as a whole, first pictured in its simpler, and then in its more complex and luxurious forms. The relation of the individual to the community is represented chiefly as one of education and training; and many strange theories—as of the equal training of men and women, and the community of wives, ideas partially drawn from Sparta—are woven into the ideal structure. Then the dialogue rises to a larger view of education, as a preparation of the soul of man, not for a community on earth, but for that heavenly life which was suggested above in the myth of the steeds.

The purely earthly unideal life is represented as a life of men tied neck and heels from birth in a cave, having their backs to the light, and their eyes fixed only on the shadows which are cast upon the wall. These they take for the only realities, and they may acquire much skill in interpreting the shadows. Turn these men suddenly to the true light, and they will be dazzled and blinded. They will feel as though they had lost the realities, and been plunged into dreams. And in pain and sorrow they will be tempted to grope back again to the familiar darkness.

Yet if they hold on in patience, and struggle up the steep till the sun himself breaks on their vision, what pain and dazzling once more, yet at the last what glorious revelation! True, if they revisit their old dwelling-place, they will not see as well as their fellows who are still living contentedly there, knowing nothing other than the shadows. They may even seem to these as dreamers who have lost their senses; and should they try to enlighten these denizens of the cave, they may be persecuted or even put to death. Such are the men who have had a sight of the heavenly verities, when compared with the children of earth and darkness.

Yet the world will never be right till those who have had this vision come back to the things of earth and order them according to the eternal verities; the philosopher must be king if ever the perfect life is to be lived on earth, either by individual or community. As it would be expressed in Scriptural language, "The kingdoms of this world must become the kingdoms of the Lord and of His Christ."

For the training of these ideal rulers an ideal education is required, which Plato calls dialectic; something of its nature is described later on, and we need not linger over it here.

The argument then seems to fall to a lower level. There are various approximations in actual experience to the ideal community, each more or less perfect according to the degree in which the good of the individual is also made the good of all, and the interests of governors and governed are alike. Parallel with each lower form of state is a lower individual nature, the worst of all being that of the tyrant, whose will is his only law, and his own self-indulgence his only motive. In him indeed Might is Right; but his life is the very antithesis of happiness. Nay, pleasure of any kind can give no law to reason; reason can judge of pleasure, but not *vice versâ*. There is no profit to a man though he gain the whole world, if *himself* be lost; if he become worse; if the better part of him be silenced and grow weaker. And after this 'fitful fever' is over, may there not be a greater bliss beyond? There have been stories told us, visions of another world, where each man is rewarded according to his works. And the book closes with a magnificent Vision of Judgment. It is the story of Er, son of Armenius, who being wounded in battle, after twelve days' trance comes back to life, and tells of the judgment seat, of heavenly bliss and hellish punishments, and of the renewal of life and the new choice given to souls not yet purified wholly of sin. "God is blameless; Man's Soul is immortal; Justice and Truth are the only things eternally good." Such is the final revelation.

The *Timaeus* is an attempt by Plato, under the guise of a Pythagorean philosopher, to image forth as in a vision or dream the actual framing of the universe, conceived as a realization of the Eternal Thought or Idea. It will be remembered that in the analysis already given of the process of knowledge in individual men, Plato found that prior to the suggestions of the senses, though not coming into consciousness except in connection with sensation, men had *ideas* that gave them a power of rendering their sensations intelligible. In the *Timaeus* Plato attempts a vision of the universe as though he saw it working itself into actuality on the lines of those ideas. The vision is briefly as follows: There is the Eternal Creator, who desired to make the world because He was good and free from jealousy, and therefore willed that all things should be like Himself; that is, that the formless, chaotic, unrealized void might receive form and order, and become, in short, real as He was. Thus creation is the process by which the Eternal Creator works out His own image, His own ideas, in and through that which is formless, that which has no name, which is nothing but possibility,—dead earth, namely, or *Matter*. And first the world-soul, image of the divine, is formed, on which as on a "diamond network" the manifold structure of things is fashioned— the stars, the seven planets with their sphere-music, the four elements, and all the various creatures, aetherial or fiery, aerial, aqueous, and earthy, with the consummation of them all in microcosm, in the animal world, and specially in man.

One can easily see that this is an attempt by Plato to carry out the reverse process in thought to that which first comes to thinking man. Man has sensations, that is, he comes first upon that which is conceivably last in creation, on the immediate and temporary things or momentary occurrences of earth. In these sensations, as they accumulate into a kind of habitual or unreasoned knowledge or opinion, he discovers elements which have been active to correlate the sensations, which have from the first exercised a governing influence upon the sensations, without which, indeed, no two sensations could be brought together to form anything one could name. These regulative, underlying, permanent elements are Ideas, *i.e.* General Forms or Notions, which, although they may come second as regards time into consciousness, are by reason known to have been there before, because through them alone can the sensations become intelligibly possible, or thinkable, or namable. Thus Plato is led to the conception of an order the reverse of our individual experience, the order of creation, the order of God's thought, which is equivalent to the order of God's working; for God's thought and God's working are inseparable.

Of course Plato, in working out his dream of creation absolutely without any scientific knowledge, the further he travels the more obviously falls into confusion and absurdity; where he touches on some ideas having a certain resemblance to modern scientific discoveries, as the law of gravitation, the circulation of the blood, the quantitative basis of differences of quality, etc., these happy guesses are apt to lead more frequently wrong than right, because they are not kept in check by any experimental tests. But taken as a 'myth,' which is perhaps all that Plato intended, the work offers much that is profoundly interesting.

With the *Timaeus* is associated another dialogue called the *Critias*, which remains only as a fragment. In it is contained a description of the celebrated visionary kingdom of Atlantis, lying far beyond the pillars of Hercules, a land of splendor and luxury and power, a land also of gentle manners and wise orderliness. "The fiction has exercised a great influence over the imagination of later ages. As many attempts have been made to find the great island as to discover the country of the lost tribes. Without regard to the description of Plato, and without a suspicion that the whole narrative is a fabrication, interpreters have looked for the spot in every part of the globe—America, Palestine, Arabia Felix, Ceylon, Sardinia, Sweden. The story had also an effect on the early navigators of the sixteenth century" (Jowett, *Plato*, vol. iii. p. 679).

CHAPTER XVI

PLATO (continued)

Metaphysics and psychology—Reason and pleasure—Criticism of the ideas—Last ideals

We now come to a series of highly important dialogues, marked as a whole by a certain diminution in the purely artistic attraction, having less of vivid characterization, less humor, less dramatic interest, less perfect construction in every way, but, on the other hand, peculiarly interesting as presenting a kind of after-criticism of his own philosophy. In them Plato brings his philosophic conceptions into striking relation with earlier or rival theories such as the Eleatic, the Megarian, the Cyrenaic, and the Cynic, and touches in these connections on many problems of deep and permanent import.

The most remarkable feature in these later dialogues is the disappearance, or even in some cases the apparently hostile criticism, of the doctrine of Ideas, and consequently of Reminiscence as the source of knowledge, and even, apparently, of Personal Immortality, so far as the doctrine of Reminiscence was imagined to guarantee it. This, however, is perhaps to push the change of view too far. We may say that Plato in these dialogues is rather the psychologist than the metaphysician; he is attempting a revised analysis of mental processes. From this point of view it was quite intelligible that he should discover difficulties in his former theory of our mental relation to the external reality, without therefore seeing reason to doubt the existence of that reality. The position is somewhat similar to that of a modern philosopher who attempts to think out the psychological problem of Human Will in relation to Almighty and Over-ruling Providence. One may very clearly see the psychological difficulties, without ceasing to believe either in the one or the other as facts.

Throughout Plato's philosophy, amidst every variation of expression, we may take these three as practically fixed points of belief or of faith, or at least of hope; *first*, that Mind is eternally master of the universe; *second*, that Man in realizing what is most truly himself is working in harmony with the Eternal Mind, and is in this way a master of nature, reason governing experience and not being a product of experience; and *thirdly* (as Socrates said before his judges), that at death we go to powers who are wise and good, and to men departed who in their day shared in the divine wisdom and goodness,—that, in short, there is something remaining for the dead, and better for those that have done good than for those that have done evil.

The first of the 'psychological dialogues,' as we have called them, is the *Philebus*. The question here is of the *summum bonum* or chief good. What is it? Is it pleasure? Is it wisdom? Or is it both? In the process of answering these questions Plato lays down rules for true definition, and establishes classifications which had an immense influence on his successor Aristotle, but which need not be further referred to here.

The general gist of the argument is as follows. Pleasure could not be regarded as a sufficient or perfect good if it was entirely emptied of the purely intellectual elements of anticipation and consciousness and memory. This would be no better than the pleasure of an oyster. On the other hand, a purely intellectual existence can hardly be regarded as perfect and sufficient either. The perfect life must be a union of both.

But this union must be an orderly and rational union; in other words, it must be one in which Mind is master and Pleasure servant; the finite, the regular, the universal must govern the indefinite, variable, particular. Thus in the perfect life there are four elements; in the body, earth, water, air, fire; in the soul, the finite, the indefinite, the union of the two, and the cause of that union. If this be so, he argues, may we not by analogy argue for a like four-fold order in the universe? There also we find regulative elements, and indefinite elements, and the union of the two. Must there not also be the Great Cause, even Divine Wisdom, ordering and governing all things?

The second of the psychological series is the *Parmenides*, in which the great Eleatic philosopher, in company with his disciple Zeno, is imagined instructing the youthful Socrates when the two were on a visit to Athens, which may or may not be historical. The most striking portion of this dialogue is the criticism already alluded to of Plato's own theory of Ideas, put into the mouth of Parmenides. Parmenides ascertains from Socrates that he is quite clear about there being Ideas of Justice, Beauty, Goodness, eternally existing, but how about Ideas of such common things as hair, mud, filth, etc.? Socrates is not so sure; to which Parmenides rejoins that as he grows older philosophy will take a surer hold of him, and that he will recognize the same law in small things and in great.

But now as to the nature of these Ideas. What, Parmenides asks, is the relation of these, as eternally existing in the mind of God, to the same ideas as possessed by individual men? Does each individual actually *partake* in the thought of God through the ideas, or are his ideas only *resemblances* of the eternal? If he partakes, then the eternal ideas are not one but many, as many as the persons who possess them. If his ideas only resemble, then there must be some basis of reference by which the resemblance is established, a *tertium quid* or third existence resembling both, and so *ad infinitum*. Socrates is puzzled by this, and suggests that perhaps the Ideas are only notions in our minds. But to this it is replied that there is an end in that case of any reality in our ideas. Unless in some way they have a true and causal relation with something beyond our minds, there is an end of mind altogether, and with mind gone everything goes.

This, as Professor Jowett remarks, "remains a difficulty for us as well as for the Greeks of the fourth century before Christ, and is the stumbling-block of Kant's *Critic*, and of the Hamiltonian adaptation of Kant as well as of the Platonic ideas. It has been said that 'you cannot criticize Revelation.' 'Then how do you know what is Revelation, or that there is one at all?' is the immediate rejoinder. 'You know nothing of things in themselves.'—'Then how do you know that there are things in themselves?' In some respects the difficulty pressed harder upon the Greek than upon ourselves. For conceiving of God more under the attribute of knowledge than we do, he was more under the necessity of separating the divine from the human, as two spheres which had no communication with one another."

Next follows an extraordinary analysis of the ideas of 'Being' and 'Unity,' remarkable not only for its subtlety, but for the relation which it historically bears to the modern philosophic system of Hegel. "Every affirmation is *ipso facto* a negation;" "the negation of a negation is an affirmation;" these are the psychological (if not metaphysical) facts, on which the analysis of Parmenides and the philosophy of Hegel are both founded.

We may pass more rapidly by the succeeding dialogues of the series: the *Theaetetus*, which is a close and powerful investigation of the nature of knowledge on familiar Platonic lines; the *Sophist*, which is an analysis of fallacious reasoning; and the *Statesman*, which, under the guise of a dialectical search for the true ruler of men, represents once more Plato's ideal of government, and contrasts this with the ignorance and charlatanism of actual politics.

In relation to subsequent psychology, and more particularly to the logical system of Aristotle, these dialogues are extremely important. We may indeed say that the systematic logic of Aristotle, as contained in the *Organon*, is little more than an abstract or digest of the logical theses of these dialogues. Definition and division, the nature and principle of classification, the theory of predication, the processes of induction and deduction, the classification and criticism of fallacies,—all these are to be found in them. The only addition really made by Aristotle was the systematic theory of the syllogism.

The *Laws*, the longest of Plato's works, seems to have been composed by him in the latest years of his long life, and was probably not published till after his death. It bears traces of its later origin in the less artful juncture of its parts, in the absence of humor, in the greater overloading of details, in the less graphic and appropriate characterization of the speakers. These speakers are three—an Athenian, a Cretan, and a Spartan. A new colony is to be led forth from Crete, and the Cretan takes advice of the others as to the ordering of the new commonwealth. We are no longer, as in *The Republic*, in an ideal world, a city coming down from, or set in, the heavens. There is no longer a perfect community; nor are philosophers to be its kings. Laws more or less similar to those of Sparta fill about half the book. But the old spirit of obedience and self-sacrifice and community is not forgotten; and on all men and women, noble and humble alike, the duty is cast, to bear in common the common burden of life.

Thus, somewhat in sadness and decay, yet with a dignity and moral grandeur not unworthy of his life's high argument, the great procession of the Ideal Philosopher's dialogues closes.

CHAPTER XVII

PLATO (concluded)

Search for universals—The thoughts of God—God cause and consummation—Dying to earth—The Platonic education

If we attempt now, by way of appendix to this very inadequate summary of the dialogues, to give in brief review some account of the main doctrines of Plato, as they may be gathered from a general view of them, we are at once met by difficulties many and serious. In the case of a genius such as Plato's, at once ironical, dramatic, and allegorical, we cannot be absolutely certain that in any given passage Plato is expressing, at all events adequately and completely, his own personal views, even at the particular stage of his own mental development then represented. And when we add to this that in a long life of unceasing intellectual development, Plato inevitably grew out of much that once satisfied him, and attained not infrequently to new points of view even of doctrines or conceptions which remained essentially unchanged, a Platonic dogma in the strict sense must clearly not be expected. One may, however, attempt in rough outline to summarize the main *tendencies* of his thought, without professing to represent its settled and authenticated results.

We may begin by an important summary of Plato's philosophy given by Aristotle (*Met.* A. 6): "In immediate succession to the Pythagorean and Eleatic philosophies came the work of Plato. In many respects his views coincided with these; in some respects, however, he is independent of the Italians. For in early youth he became a student of Cratylus and of the school of Heraclitus, and accepted from them the view that the objects of sense are in eternal flux, and that of these, therefore, there can be no absolute knowledge. Then came Socrates, who busied himself only with questions of morals, and not at all with the world of physics. But in his ethical inquiries his search was ever for universals, and he was the first to set his mind to the discovery of definitions. Plato following him in this, came to the conclusion that these universals could not belong to the things of sense, which were ever changing, but to some other kind of existences. Thus he came to conceive of universals as forms or *ideas* of real existences, by reference to which, and in consequence of analogies to which, the things of sense in every case received their names, and became thinkable objects."

From this it followed to Plato that in so far as the senses took an illusive appearance of themselves giving the knowledge which really was supplied by reason as the organ of ideas, in the same degree the body which is the instrument of sense can only be a source of illusion and a hindrance to knowledge. The wise man, therefore, will seek to free himself from the bonds of the body, and die while he lives by philosophic contemplation, free as far as possible from the disturbing influence of the senses. This process of *rational* realization Plato called Dialectic. The objects contemplated by the reason, brought into consciousness on the occurrence of sensible perception, but never caused by these, were not mere notions in the mind of the individual thinker, nor were they mere properties of individual things; this would be to make an end of science on the one hand, of reality on the other. Nor had they existence in any mere place, not even beyond the heavens. Their home was Mind, not this mind or that, but Mind Universal, which is God.

In these 'thoughts of God' was the root or essence which gave reality to the things of sense; they were the Unity which realized itself in multiplicity. It is because things partake of the Idea that we give them a name. The thing as such is seen, not known; the idea as such is known, not seen.

The whole conception of Plato in this connection is based on the assumption that there is such a thing as knowledge. If all things are ever in change, then knowledge is impossible; but conversely, if there is such a thing as knowledge, then there must be a continuing object of knowledge; and beauty, goodness, reality are then no dreams. The process of apprehension of these 'thoughts of God,' these eternal objects of knowledge, whether occasioned by sensation or not, is essentially a process of self-inquiry, or, as he in one stage called it, of Reminiscence. The process is the same in essence, whether going on in thought or expressed in speech; it is a process of *naming*. Not that names ever resemble realities fully; they are only approximations, limited by the conditions of human error and human convention. There is nevertheless an inter-communion between ideas and things. We must neither go entirely with those who affirm the one (the Eleatics), nor with those who affirm the many (the Heracliteans), but accept both. There is a union in all that exists both of That Which *Is*, and of that concerning which all we can say is that it is *Other* than what is. This 'Other,' through union with what is, attains to being of a kind; while on the other hand, What Is by union with the 'Other' attains to variety, and thus more fully realizes itself.

That which Plato here calls 'What Is' he elsewhere calls 'The Limiting or Defining'; the 'Other' he calls 'The Unlimited or Undefined.' Each has a function in the divine process. The thoughts of God attain realization in the world of things which change and pass, through the infusion of themselves in, or the superimposing of themselves upon, that which is Nothing apart from them,—the mere negation of what is, and yet necessary as the 'Other' or correlative of what is. Thus we get, in fact, *four* forms of existence: there is the Idea or Limiting (apart); there is the Negative or Unlimited (apart), there is the Union of the two (represented in language by subject and predicate), which as a whole is this frame of things as we know it; and fourthly, there is the *Cause* of the Union, which is God. And God is cause not only as the beginning of all things, but also as the measure and law of their perfection, and the end towards which they go. He is the Good, and the cause of Good, and the consummation and realization of Good.

This absolute Being, this perfect Good, we cannot see, blinded as we are, like men that have been dwelling in a cave, by excess of light. We must, therefore, look on Him indirectly, as on an image of Him, in our own souls and in the world, in so far as in either we discern, by reason, that which is rational and good.

Thus God is not only the cause and the end of all good, He is also the cause and the end of all knowledge. Even as the sun is not only the most glorious of all visible objects, but is also the cause of the life and beauty of all other things, and the provider of the light whereby we see them, so also is it for the eye of the soul. God is its light, God is the most glorious object of its contemplation, God we behold imaged forth in all the objects which the soul by reason contemplates.

The ideas whereof the 'Other' (or, as he again calls it, the 'Great and Small' or 'More and Less,' meaning that which is unnamable, or wholly neutral in character, and which may therefore be represented equally by contradictory attributes) by participation becomes a resemblance, Plato compared to the 'Numbers' of the Pythagoreans. Hence, Aristotle remarks (*Met.* A. 6), Plato found in the ideas the originative or formative Cause of things, that which made them what they were or could be called,—their *Essence*; in the 'Great and Small' he found the opposite principle or *Matter* (Raw Material) of things.

In this way the antithesis of Mind and Matter, whether on the great scale in creation or on the small in rational perception, is not an antithesis of unrelated opposition. Each is correlative of the other, so to speak as the male and the female; the one is generative, formative, active, positive; the other is capable of being impregnated, receptive, passive, negative; but neither can realize itself apart from the other.

This relation of 'Being' with that which is 'Other than Being' is Creation, wherein we can conceive of the world as coming to be, yet not in Time. And in the same way Plato speaks of a third form, besides the Idea and that which receives it, namely, 'Formless Space, the mother of all things.' As Kant might have formulated it, Time and Space are not prior to creation, they are forms under which creation becomes thinkable.

The 'Other' or Negative element, Plato more or less vaguely connected with the evil that is in the world. This evil we can never expect to perish utterly from the world; it must ever be here as the antithesis of the good. But with the gods it dwells not; here in this mortal nature, and in this region of mingling, it must of necessity still be found. The wise man will therefore seek to die to the evil, and while yet in this world of mortality, to think immortal things, and so as far as may be flee from the evil. Thereby shall he liken himself to the divine. For it is a likening to the divine to be just and holy and true.

This, then, is the *summum bonum*, the end of life. For as the excellence or end of any organ or instrument consists in that perfection of its parts, whereby each separately and the whole together work well towards the fulfilling of that which it is designed to accomplish, so the excellence of man must consist in a perfect ordering of all his parts to the perfect working of his whole organism as a rational being. The faculties of man are three: the Desire of the body, the Passion of the heart, the Thought of the soul; the perfect working of all three, Temperance, Courage, Wisdom, and consequently the perfect working of the whole man, is Righteousness. From this springs that ordered tranquility which is at once true happiness and perfect virtue.

Yet since individual men are not self-sufficient, but have separate capacities, and a need of union for mutual help and comfort, the perfect realization of this virtue can only be in a perfect civic community. And corresponding with the three parts of the man there will be three orders in the community: the Workers and Traders, the Soldiers, and the Ruling or Guardian class. When all these perform their proper functions in perfect harmony, then is the perfection of the whole realized, in Civic Excellence or Justice.

To this end a careful civic education is necessary, *first*, because to *know* what is for the general good is difficult, for we have to learn not only in general but in detail that even the individual good can be secured only through the general; and *second*, because few, if any, are capable of seeking the general good, even if they know it, without the guidance of discipline and the restraints of law. Thus, with a view to its own perfection, and the good of all its members, Education is the chief work of the State.

It will be remembered (see foregoing page) that in Plato's division of the soul of man there are three faculties, Desire, Passion, Reason; in the division of the soul's perfection three corresponding virtues, Temperance, Courage, Wisdom; and in the division of the state three corresponding orders, Traders, Soldiers, Guardians. So in Education there are three stages. First, *Music* (including all manner of artistic and refining influences), whose function it is so to attemper the desires of the heart that all animalism and sensualism may be eliminated, and only the love and longing for that which is lovely and of good report may remain. Second, *Gymnastic*, whose function it is through ordered labor and suffering so to subdue and rationalize the passionate part of the soul, that it may become the willing and obedient servant of that which is just and true. And third, *Mathematics*, by which the rational element of the soul may be trained to realize itself, being weaned, by the ordered apprehension of the 'diamond net' of laws which underlie all the phenomena of nature, away from the mere surface appearances of things, the accidental, individual, momentary,—to the deep-seated realities, which are necessary, universal, eternal.

And just as there was a perfectness of the soul transcending all particular virtues, whether of Temperance or Courage or Wisdom, namely, that absolute Rightness or Righteousness which gathered them all into itself, so at the end of these three stages of education there is a higher mood of thought, wherein the soul, purified, chastened, enlightened, in communing with itself through *Dialectic* (the Socratic art of questioning transfigured) communes also with the Divine, and in thinking out its own deepest thoughts, thinks out the thoughts of the great Creator Himself, becomes one with Him, finds its final realization through absorption into Him, and in His light sees light.

CHAPTER XVIII

ARISTOTLE

An unruly pupil—The philosopher's library—The predominance of Aristotle—Relation to Plato—The highest philosophy—Ideas and things—The true realism

Plato before his death bequeathed his Academy to his nephew Speusippus, who continued its president for eight years; and on his death the office passed to Xenocrates, who held it for twenty-five years. From him it passed in succession to Polemo, Crates, Crantor, and others. Plato was thus the founder of a school or sect of teachers who busied themselves with commenting, expanding, modifying here and there the doctrines of the master. Little of their works beyond the names has been preserved, and indeed we can hardly regret the loss. These men no doubt did much to popularize the thoughts of their master, and in this way largely influenced the later development of philosophy; but they had nothing substantial to add, and so the stern pruning-hook of time has cut them off from remembrance.

Aristotle was the son of a Greek physician, member of the colony of Stagira in Thrace. His father, Nicomachus by name, was a man of such eminence in his profession as to hold the post of physician to Amyntas, king of Macedonia, father of Philip the subverter of Greek freedom. Not only was his father an expert physician, he was also a student of natural history, and wrote several works on the subject. We shall find that the fresh element which Aristotle brought to the Academic philosophy was in a very great measure just that minute attention to details and keen apprehension of vital phenomena which we may consider he inherited from his father. He was born 384 B.C., and on the death of his father, in his eighteenth year, he came to Athens, and became a student of philosophy under Plato, whose pupil he continued to be for twenty years,—indeed till the death of the master. That he, undoubtedly a far greater man than Speusippus or Xenocrates, should not have been nominated to the succession has been variously explained; he is said to have been lacking in respect and gratitude to the master; Plato is said to have remarked of him that he needed the curb as much as Xenocrates needed the spur. The facts really need no explanation. The original genius is never sufficiently subordinate and amenable to discipline. He is apt to be critical, to startle his easy-going companions with new and seemingly heterodox views, he is the 'ugly duckling' whom all the virtuous and commonplace brood must cackle at. The Academy, when its great master died, was no place for Aristotle. He retired to Atarneus, a city of Mysia opposite to Lesbos, where a friend named Hermias was tyrant, and there he married Hermias' niece. After staying at Atarneus some three years he was invited by Philip, now king of Macedon, to undertake the instruction of his son Alexander, the future conqueror, who was then thirteen years old. He remained with Alexander for eight years, though of course he could hardly be regarded as Alexander's tutor during all that time, since Alexander at a very early age was called to take a part in public affairs. However a strong friendship was formed between the philosopher and the young prince, and in after years Alexander loaded his former master with benefits. Even while on his march of conquest through Asia he did not forget him, but sent him from every country through which he passed specimens which might help him in his projected History of Animals, as well as an enormous sum of money to aid him in his investigations.

After the death of Philip, Aristotle returned to Athens, and opened a school of philosophy on his own account in the Lyceum. Here some authorities tell us he lectured to his pupils while he paced up and down before them; hence the epithet applied to the school, the *Peripatetics*. Probably, however, the name is derived from the 'Peripati' or covered walks in the neighbourhood of that temple in which he taught. He devoted his mornings to lectures of a more philosophical and technical character; to these only the abler and more advanced students were admitted. In the afternoons he lectured on subjects of a more popular kind—rhetoric, the art of politics, etc.—to larger audiences. Corresponding with this division, he also was in the habit of classifying his writings as Acroatic or technical, and Exoteric or popular. He accumulated a large library and museum, to which he contributed an astonishing number of works of his own, on every conceivable branch of knowledge.

The after history of Aristotle's library, including the MSS. of his own works, is interesting and even romantic. Aristotle's successor in the school was Theophrastus, who added to the library bequeathed him by Aristotle many works of his own, and others purchased by him. Theophrastus bequeathed the entire library to Neleus, his friend and pupil, who, on leaving Athens to reside at Scepsis in the Troad, took the library with him. There it remained for nearly two hundred years in possession of the Neleus family, who kept the collection hidden in a cellar for fear it should be seized to increase the royal library of Pergamus. In such a situation the works suffered much harm from worms and damp, till at last (*circa* 100 B.C.) they were brought out and sold to one Apellicon, a rich gentleman resident in Athens, himself a member of the Peripatetic school. In 86 B.C. Sulla, the Roman dictator, besieged and captured Athens, and among other prizes conveyed the library of Apellicon to Rome, and thus many of the most important works of Aristotle for the first time were made known to the Roman and Alexandrian schools. It is a curious circumstance that the philosopher whose influence was destined to be paramount for more than a thousand years in the Christian era, was thus deprived by accident of his legitimate importance in the centuries immediately following his own.

But his temporary and accidental eclipse was amply compensated in the effect upon the civilized world which he subsequently exercised. So all-embracing, so systematic, so absolutely complete did his philosophy appear, that he seemed to after generations to have left nothing more to discover. He at once attained a supremacy which lasted for some two thousand years, not only over the Greek-speaking world, but over every form of the civilization of that long period, Greek, Roman, Syrian, Arabic, from the Euphrates to the Atlantic, from Africa to Britain. His authority was accepted equally by the learned doctors of Moorish Cordova and the Fathers of the Church; to know Aristotle was to have all knowledge; not to know him was to be a boor; to deny him was to be a heretic.

His style has nothing of the grace of Plato; he illuminates his works with no myths or allegories; his manner is dry, sententious, familiar, without the slightest attempt at ornament. There are occasional touches of caustic humor, but nothing of emotion, still less of rhapsody. His strength lies in the vast architectonic genius by which he correlates every domain of the knowable in a single scheme, and in the extraordinary faculty for illustrative detail with which he fills the scheme in every part. He knows, and can shrewdly criticize every thinker and writer who has preceded him; he classifies them as he classifies the mental faculties, the parts of logical speech, the parts of sophistry, the parts of rhetoric, the parts of animals, the parts of the soul, the parts of the state; he defines, distinguishes, combines, classifies, with the same sureness and minuteness of method in them all. He can start from a general conception, expand it into its parts, separate these again by distinguishing details till he brings the matter down to its lowest possible terms, or *infimae species*. Or he can start from these, find analogies among them constituting more general species, and so in ascending scale travel surely up to a general conception, or *summum genus*.

In his general conception of philosophy he was to a large extent in agreement with Plato; but he endeavored to attain to a more technical precision; he sought to systematize into greater completeness; he pared off everything which he considered merely metaphorical or fanciful, and therefore non-essential. The operations of nature, the phenomena of life, were used in a much fuller and more definite way to illustrate or even formulate the theory; but in its main ideas Aristotle's philosophy is Plato's philosophy. The one clothed it in poetry, the other in formulae; the one had a more entrancing vision, the other a clearer and more exact apprehension; but there is no essential divergence.

Aristotle's account of the origin or foundation of philosophy is as follows (*Met.* A. 2): "Wonder is and always has been the first incentive to philosophy. At first men wondered at what puzzled them near at hand, then by gradual advance they came to notice and wonder at things still greater, as at the phases of the moon, the eclipses of sun and moon, the wonders of the stars, and the origin of the universe. Now he who is puzzled and in a maze regards himself as a know-nothing; wherefore the philosopher is apt to be fond of wondrous tales or myths. And inasmuch as it was a consciousness of ignorance that drove men to philosophy, it is for the correction of this ignorance, and not for any material utility, that the pursuit of knowledge exists. Indeed it is, as a rule, only when all other wants are well supplied that, by way of ease and recreation, men turn to this inquiry. And thus, since no satisfaction beyond itself is sought by philosophy, we speak of it as we speak of the freeman. We call that man free whose existence is for himself and not for another; so also philosophy is of all the sciences the only one that is free, for it alone exists for itself.

"Moreover, this philosophy, which is the investigation of the first causes of things, is the most truly educative among the sciences. For instructors are persons who show us the causes of things. And knowledge for the sake of knowledge belongs most properly to that inquiry which deals with what is most truly a matter of knowledge. For he who is seeking knowledge for its own sake will choose to have that knowledge which most truly deserves the name, the knowledge, namely, of what most truly appertains to knowledge. Now the things that most truly appertain to knowledge are the first causes; for in virtue of one's possession of these, and by deduction from these, all else comes to be known; we do not come to know them through what is inferior to them and underlying them. . . . The wise man ought therefore to know not only those things which are the outcome and product of first causes, he must be possessed of the truth as to the first causes themselves. And wisdom indeed is just this thoughtful science, a science of what is highest, not truncated of its head."

"To the man, therefore, who has in fullest measure this knowledge of universals, all knowledge must lie to hand; for in a way he knows all that underlies them. Yet in a sense these universals are what men find hardest to apprehend, because they stand at the furthest extremity from the perceptions of sense."

"Yet if anything exist which is eternal, immovable, freed from gross matter, the contemplative science alone can apprehend this. Physical science certainly cannot, for physics is of that which is ever in flux; nor can mathematical science apprehend it; we must look to a mode of science prior to and higher than both. The objects of physics are neither unchangeable nor free from matter; the objects of mathematics are indeed unchangeable, but we can hardly say they are free from matter; they have certainly relations with matter. But the first and highest science has to do with that which is unmoved and apart from matter; its function is with the eternal first causes of things. There are therefore three modes of theoretical inquiry: the science of physics, the science of mathematics, the science of God. For it is clear that if the divine is anywhere, it must be in that form of existence I have spoken of (*i.e.* in first causes). . . . If, therefore, there be any form of existence immovable, this we must regard as prior, and the philosophy of this we must consider the first philosophy, universal for the same reason that it is first. It deals with existence as such, inquiring what it is and what are its attributes as pure existence."

This is somewhat more technical than the language of Plato, but if we compare it with what was said above we shall find an essential identity. Yet Aristotle frequently impugns Plato's doctrine of ideas, sometimes on the lines already taken by Plato himself, sometimes in other ways. Thus (*Met. Z.* 15, 16) he says: "That which is *one* cannot be in many places at one time, but that which is common or general is in many places at one time. Hence it follows that no universal exists apart from the individual things. But those who hold the doctrine of ideas, on one side are right, viz. in maintaining their separate existence, if they are to be substances or existences at all. On the other side they are wrong, because by the idea or form which they maintain to be separate they mean the one attribute predicable of many things. The reason why they do this is because they cannot indicate what these supposed imperishable essences are, apart from the individual substances which are the objects of perception. The result is that they simply represent them under the same forms as those of the perishable objects of sensation which are familiar to our senses, with the addition of a phrase—*i.e.* they say 'man as such,' 'horse as such,' or 'the absolute man,' 'the absolute horse.'"

Aristotle here makes a point against Plato and his school, inasmuch as, starting from the assumption that of the world of sense there could be no knowledge, no apprehension fixed or certain, and setting over against this a world of general forms which were fixed and certain, they had nothing with which to fill this second supposed world except the data of sense as found in individuals. Plato's mistake was in confusing the mere 'this,' which is the conceived starting-point of any sensation, but which, like a mathematical point, has nothing which can be said about it, with individual objects as they exist and are known in all the manifold and, in fact, infinite relations of reality. The bare subject 'this' presents at the one extreme the same emptiness, the same mere possibility of knowledge, which is presented at the other by the bare predicate 'is.' But Plato, having an objection to the former, as representing to him the merely physical and therefore the passing and unreal, clothes it for the nonce in the various attributes which are ordinarily associated with it when we say, 'this man,' 'this horse,' only to strip them off successively as data of sensation, and so at last get, by an illusory process of abstraction and generalization, to the ultimate generality of being, which is the mere 'is' of bare predication converted into a supposed eternal substance.

Aristotle was as convinced as Plato that there must be some fixed and immovable object or reality corresponding to true and certain knowledge, but with his scientific instincts he was not content to have it left in a condition of emptiness, attractive enough to the more emotional and imaginative Plato. And hence we have elsewhere quite as strong and definite statements as those quoted above about universals, to the effect that existence is in the fullest and most real sense to be predicated of *individual* things, and that only in a secondary sense can existence be predicated of universals, in virtue of their being found in individual things. Moreover, among universals the *species*, he maintains, has more of existence in it than the genus, because it is nearer to the individual or primary existence. For if you predicate of an individual thing of what species it is, you supply a statement more full of information and more closely connected with the thing than if you predicate to what genus it belongs; for example, if asked, "What is this?" and you answer, "A man," you give more information than if you say, "A living creature."

How did Aristotle reconcile these two points of view, the one, in which he conceives thought as starting from first causes, the most universal objects of knowledge, and descending to particulars; the other, in which thought starts from the individual objects, and predicates of them by apprehension of their properties? The antithesis is no accidental one; on the contrary, it is the governing idea of his Logic, with its ascending process or Induction, and its descending process or Syllogism. Was thought a mere process in an unmeaning circle, the 'upward and downward way' of Plato?

As to this we may answer first that while formally Aristotle displays much the same 'dualism' or unreconciled separation of the 'thing' and the 'idea' as Plato, his practical sense and his scientific instincts led him to occupy himself largely not with either the empty 'thing' or the equally empty 'idea,' but with the true *individuals*, which are at the same time the true universals, namely, real objects as known, having, so far as they are known, certain forms or categories under which you can class them, having, so far as they are not yet fully known, a certain raw material for further inquiry through observation. In this way Thought and Matter, instead of being in eternal and irreconcilable antagonism as the Real and the Unreal, become parts of the same reality, the first summing up the knowledge of things already attained, the second symbolizing the infinite possibilities of further ascertainment. And thus the word 'Matter' is applied by Aristotle to the highest genus, as the relatively indefinite compared with the more fully defined species included under it; it is also applied by him to the individual object, in so far as that object contains qualities not yet fully brought into predication.

And second, we observe that Aristotle introduced a new conception which to his view established a *vital relation* between the universal and the individual. This conception he formulated in the correlatives, *Potentiality* and *Actuality*. With these he closely connected the idea of *Final Cause*. The three to Aristotle constituted a single reality; they are organically correlative. In a living creature we find a number of members or organs all closely interdependent and mutually conditioning each other. Each has its separate function, yet none of them can perform its particular function well unless all the others are performing theirs well, and the effect of the right performance of function by each is to enable the others also to perform theirs. The total result of all these mutually related functions is *Life*; this is their End or Final Cause, which does not exist apart from them, but is constituted at every moment by them. This Life is at the same time the condition on which alone each and every one of the functions constituting it can be performed. Thus life in an organism is at once the end and the middle and the beginning; it is the cause final, the cause formal, the cause efficient. Life then is an *Entelechy*, as Aristotle calls it, by which he means the realization in unity of the total activities exhibited in the members of the living organism.

In such an existence every part is at once a potentiality and an actuality, and so also is the whole. We can begin anywhere and travel out from that point to the whole; we can take the whole and find in it all the parts.

CHAPTER XIX

ARISTOTLE (*continued*)

Realization and reminiscence—The crux of philosophy—Reason in education—The chief good—Origin of communities

If we look closely at this conception of Aristotle's we shall see that it has a nearer relation to the Platonic doctrine of Ideas, and even to the doctrine of Reminiscence, than perhaps even Aristotle himself realized. The fundamental conception of Plato, it will be remembered, is that of an eternally existing 'thought of God,' in manifold forms or 'ideas,' which come into the consciousness of men in connection with or on occasion of sensations, which are therefore in our experience later than the sensations, but which we nevertheless by reason recognize as necessarily prior to the sensations, inasmuch as it is through these ideas alone that the sensations are knowable or namable at all. Thus the final end for man is by contemplation and 'daily dying to the world of sense,' to come at last into the full inheritance in conscious knowledge of that 'thought of God' which was latent from the first in his soul, and of which in its fullness God Himself is eternally and necessarily possessed.

This is really Aristotle's idea, only Plato expresses it rather under a psychological, Aristotle under a vital, formula. God, Aristotle says, is eternally and necessarily Entelechy, absolute realization. *To us*, that which is first *in time* (the individual perception) is not first in *essence*, or absolutely. What is first in essence or absolutely, is the universal, that is, the form or idea, the datum of reason. And this distinction between time and the absolute, between our individual experience and the essential or ultimate reality, runs all through the philosophy of Aristotle. The 'Realization' of Aristotle is the 'Reminiscence' of Plato.

This conception Aristotle extended to Thought, to the various forms of life, to education, to morals, to politics.

Thought is an entelechy, an organic whole, in which every process conditions and is conditioned by every other. If we begin with sensation, the sensation, blank as regards predication, has relations to that which is infinitely real,—the object, the real thing before us,—which relations science will never exhaust. If we start from the other end, with the datum of thought, consciousness, existence, mind, this is equally blank as regards predication, yet it has relations to another existence infinitely real,—the subject that thinks,—which relations religion and morality and sentiment and love will never exhaust. Or, as Aristotle and as common sense prefers to do, if we, with our developed habits of thought and our store of accumulated information, choose to deal with things from a basis midway between the two extremes, in the ordinary way of ordinary people, we shall find both processes working simultaneously and in organic correlation. That is to say, we shall be increasing the *individuality* of the objects known, by the operation of true thought and observation in the discovery of new characters or qualities in them; we shall be increasing by the same act the *generality* of the objects known, by the discovery of new relations, new genera under which to bring them. Individualization and generalization are only opposed, as mutually conditioning factors of the same organic function.

This analysis of thought must be regarded rather as a paraphrase of Aristotle than as a literal transcript. He is hesitating and obscure, and at times apparently self-contradictory. He has not, any more than Plato, quite cleared himself of the confusion between the mutually contrary individual and universal in *propositions*, and the organically correlative individual and universal in *things as known*. But on the whole the tendency of his analysis is towards an apprehension of the true realism, which neither denies matter in favor of mind nor mind in favor of matter, but recognizes that both mind and matter are organically correlated, and ultimately identical.

The crux of philosophy, so far as thus apprehended by Aristotle, is no longer in the supposed dualism of mind and matter, but there is a crux still. What is the meaning of this 'Ultimately'? Or, putting it in Aristotle's formula, Why this relation of potentiality and actuality? Why this eternal coming to be, even if the coming to be is no unreasoned accident, but a coming to be of that which is vitally or in germ *there*? Or theologically, Why did God make the world? Why this groaning and travailing of the creature? Why this eternal 'By and by' wherein all sin is to disappear, all sorrow to be consoled, all the clashings and the infinite deceptions of life to be stilled and satisfied? An illustration of Aristotle's attempt to answer this question will be given later on. That the answer is a failure need not surprise us. If we even now 'see only as in a glass darkly' on such a question, we need not blame Plato or Aristotle for not seeing 'face to face.'

Life is an entelechy, not only abstractedly, as already shown, but in respect of the varieties of its manifestations. We pass from the elementary life of mere growth common to plants and animals, to the animal life of impulse and sensation, thence we rise still higher to the life of rational action which is the peculiar function of man. Each is a *potentiality* to that which is immediately above it; in other words, each contains in germ the possibilities which are realized in that stage which is higher. Thus is there a touch of nature which makes the whole world kin, a purpose running through all the manifestations of life; each is a preparation for something higher.

Education is in like manner an entelechy. For what is the *differentia*, the distinguishing character of the life of man? Aristotle answers, the possession of reason. It is the action of reason upon the desires that raises the life of man above the brutes. This, observe, is not the restraining action of something wholly alien to the desires, which is too often how Plato represents the matter. This would be to lose the dynamic idea. The desires, as Aristotle generally conceives them, are there in the animal life, prepared, so to speak, to receive the organic perfection which reason alone can give them. Intellect, on the other hand, is equally in need of the desires, for thought without desire cannot supply motive. If intellect is *logos* or reason, desire is that which is fitted to be obedient to reason.

It will be remembered that the question to which Plato addressed himself in one of his earlier dialogues, already frequently referred to, the *Meno*, was the teachableness of Virtue; in that dialogue he comes to the conclusion that Virtue is teachable, but that there are none capable of teaching it; for the wise men of the time are guided not by knowledge but by right opinion, or by a divine instinct which is incommunicable. Plato is thus led to seek a machinery of education, and it is with a view to this that he constructs his ideal *Republic*. Aristotle took up this view of the state as educative of the individual citizens, and brought it under the dynamic formula. In the child reason is not actual; there is no rational law governing his acts, these are the immediate result of the strongest impulse. Yet only when a succession of virtuous acts has formed the virtuous habit can a man be said to be truly good. How is this process to begin? The answer is that the reason which is only latent or dynamic in the child is actual or realized in the parent or teacher, or generally in the community which educates the child. The law at first then is imposed on the child from without, it has an appearance of unnaturalness, but only an appearance. For the law is there in the child, prepared, as he goes on in obedience, gradually to answer from within to the summons from without, till along with the virtuous habit there emerges also into the consciousness of the child, no longer a child but a man, the apprehension of the law as his own truest nature.

These remarks on education are sufficient to show that in Morals also, as conceived by Aristotle, there is a law of vital development. It may be sufficient by way of illustration to quote the introductory sentences of Aristotle's *Ethics*, in which the question of the nature of the chief good is, in his usual tentative manner, discussed: "If there be any end of what we do which we desire for itself, while all other ends are desired for it, that is, if we do not in every case have some ulterior end (for if that were so we should go on to infinity, and our efforts would be vain and useless), this ultimate end desired for itself will clearly be the chief good and the ultimate best. Now since every activity, whether of knowing or doing, aims at some good, it is for us to settle what the good is which the civic activity aims at,—what, in short, is the ultimate end of all 'goods' connected with conduct? So far as the name goes all are pretty well agreed as to the answer; gentle and simple alike declare it to be happiness, involving, however, in their minds on the one hand well-living, on the other hand, well-doing. When you ask them, however, to define this happiness more exactly, you find that opinions are divided, and the many and the philosophers have different answers.

"But if you ask a musician or a sculptor or any man of skill, any person, in fact, who has some special work and activity, what the chief good is for him, he will tell you that the chief good is in the work well done. If then man has any special work or function, we may assume that the chief good for man will be in the well-doing of that function. What now is man's special function? It cannot be mere living, for that he has in common with plants, and we are seeking what is peculiar to him. The mere life of nurture and growth must therefore be put on one side. We come next to life as sensitive to pleasure and pain. But this man shares with the horse, the ox, and other animals. What remains is the life of action of a reasonable being. Now of reason as it is in man there are two parts, one obeying, one possessing and considering. And there are also two aspects in which the active or moral life may be taken, one potential, one actual. Clearly for our definition of the chief good we must take the moral life in its full actual realization, since this is superior to the other.

"If our view thus far be correct, it follows that the chief good for man consists in the full realization and perfection of the life of man as man, in accordance with the specific excellence belonging to that life, and if there be more specific excellences than one, then in accordance with that excellence which is the best and the most rounded or complete. We must add, however, the qualification, 'in a rounded life.' For one swallow does not make a summer, nor yet one day. And so one day or some brief period of attainment is not sufficient to make a man happy and blest."

The close relation of this to the teaching of Socrates and Plato need hardly be insisted on, or the way in which he correlates their ideas with his own conception of an actualized perfection.

Aristotle then proceeds to a definition of the 'specific excellence' or virtue of man, which is to be the standard by which we decide how far he has fully and perfectly realized the possibilities of his being. To this end he distinguishes in man's nature three modes of existence: first, *feelings* such as joy, pain, anger; second, *potentialities* or capacities for such feelings; third, *habits* which are built upon these potentialities, but with an element of reason or deliberation superadded. He has no difficulty in establishing that the virtue of man must be a habit. And the test of the excellence of that habit, as of every other developed capacity, will be twofold; it will make the worker good, it will cause him to produce good work.

So far Aristotle's analysis of virtue is quite on the lines of his general philosophy. Here, however, he diverges into what seems at first a curiously mechanical conception. Pointing out that in everything quantitative there are two extremes conceivable, and a *mean* or average between them, he proceeds to define virtue as a mean between two extremes, a mean, however, having relation to no mere numerical standard, but having reference *to us*. In this last qualification he perhaps saves his definition from its mechanical turn, while he leaves himself scope for much curious and ingenious observation on the several virtues regarded as means between two extremes. He further endeavors to save it by adding, that it is "defined by reason, and as the wise man would define it."

Reason then, as the impersonal ruler,—the wise man, as the personification of reason,—this is the standard of virtue, and therefore also of happiness. How then shall we escape an externality in our standard, divesting it of that binding character which comes only when the law without is also recognized and accepted as the law within? The answer of Aristotle, as of his predecessors, is that this will be brought about by wise training and virtuous surroundings, in short, by the civic community being itself good and happy. Thus we get another dynamic relation;

for regarded as a member of the body politic each individual becomes a potentiality along with all the other members, conditioned by the state of which he and they are members, brought gradually into harmony with the reason which is in the state, and in the process realizing not his own possibilities only, but those of the community also, which exists only in and through its members. Thus each and all, in so far as they realize their own well-being by the perfect development of the virtuous habit in their lives, contribute *ipso facto* to the supreme end of the state, which is the perfect realization of the whole possibilities of the total organism, and consequently of every member of it.

The *State* therefore is also an entelechy. For man is not made to dwell alone. "There is first the fact of sex; then the fact of children; third, the fact of variety of capacity, implying variety of position, some having greater powers of wisdom and forethought, and being therefore naturally the rulers; others having bodily powers suitable for carrying out the rulers' designs, and being therefore naturally subjects. Thus we have as a first or simplest community the family, next the village, then the full or perfect state, which, seeking to realize an absolute self-sufficiency within itself, rises from mere living to well-living as an aim of existence. This higher existence is as natural and necessary as any simpler form, being, in fact, the end or final and necessary perfection of all such lower forms of existence. Man therefore is by the natural necessity of his being a 'political animal,' and he who is not a citizen,—that is, by reason of something peculiar in his nature and not by a mere accident,—must either be deficient or something superhuman. And while man is the noblest of animals when thus fully perfected in an ordered community, on the other hand when deprived of law and justice he is the very worst. For there is nothing so dreadful as lawlessness armed. And man is born with the arms of thought and special capacities or excellences, which it is quite possible for him to use for other and contrary purposes. And therefore man is the most wicked and cruel animal living when he is vicious, the most lustful and the most gluttonous. The justice which restrains all this is a civic quality; and law is the orderly arrangement of the civic community" (Arist. *Pol.* i. p. 2).

CHAPTER XX

ARISTOTLE (*concluded*)

God and necessity—The vital principle—Soul as realization—Function and capacity—His method

Throughout Aristotle's physical philosophy the same conception runs: "All animals in their fully developed state require two members above all—one whereby to take in nourishment, the other whereby to get rid of what is superfluous. For no animal can exist or grow without nourishment. And there is a third member in them all half-way between these, in which resides the principle of their life. This is the heart, which all blood-possessing animals have. From it comes the arterial system which Nature has made hollow to contain the liquid blood. The situation of the heart is a commanding one, being near the middle and rather above than below, and rather towards the front than the back. For Nature ever establishes that which is most honorable in the most honorable places, unless some supreme necessity overrules. We see this most clearly in the case of man; but the same tendency for the heart to occupy the centre is seen also in other animals, when we regard only that portion of their body which is essential, and the limit of this is at the place where superfluities are removed. The limbs are arranged differently in different animals, and are not among the parts essential to life; consequently animals may live even if these are removed. . . . Anaxagoras says that man is the wisest of animals because he possesses hands. It would be more reasonable to say that he possesses hands because he is the wisest. For the hands are an instrument; and Nature always assigns an instrument to the one fitted to use it, just as a sensible man would. For it is more reasonable to give a flute to a flute-player than to confer on a man who has some flutes the art of playing them. To that which is the greater and higher she adds what is less important, and not *vice versâ*. Therefore to the creature fitted to acquire the largest number of skills Nature assigned the hand, the instrument useful for the largest number of purposes" (Arist. *De Part. An.* iv. p. 10).

And in the macrocosm, the visible and invisible world about us, the same conception holds: "The existence of God is an eternally perfect entelechy, a life everlasting. In that, therefore, which belongs to the divine there must be an eternally perfect movement. Therefore the heavens, which are as it were the body of the Divine, are in form a sphere, of necessity ever in circular motion. Why then is not this true of every portion of the universe? Because there must of necessity be a point of rest of the circling body at the centre. Yet the circling body cannot rest either as a whole or as regards any part of it, otherwise its motion could not be eternal, which by nature it is. Now that which is a violation of nature cannot be eternal, but the violation is posterior to that which is in accordance with nature, and thus the unnatural is a kind of displacement or degeneracy from the natural, taking the form of a coming into being.

"Necessity then requires earth, as the element standing still at the centre. Now if there must be earth, there must be fire. For if one of two opposites is natural or necessary, the other must be necessary too, each, in fact, implying the necessity of the other. For the two have the same substantial basis, only the positive form is naturally prior to the negative; for instance, warm is prior to cold. And in the same way motionlessness and heaviness are predicated in virtue of the absence of motion and lightness, *i.e.* the latter are essentially prior.

"Further, if there are fire and earth, there must also be the elements which lie between these, each having an antithetic relation to each. From this it follows that there must be a process of coming into being, because none of these elements can be eternal, but each affects, and is affected by each, and they are mutually destructive. Now it is not to be argued that anything which can be moved can be eternal, except in the case of that which by its own nature has eternal motion. And if coming into being must be predicated of these, then other forms of change can also be predicated" (Arist. *De Coelo*, ii. p. 3).

This passage is worth quoting as illustrating, not only Aristotle's conception of the divine entelechy, but also the ingenuity with which he gave that appearance of logical completeness to the vague and ill-digested scientific imaginations of the time, which remained so evil an inheritance for thousands of years. It is to be observed, in order to complete Aristotle's theory on this subject, that the four elements, Earth, Water, Air, Fire, are all equally in a world which is "contrary to nature," that is, the world of change, of coming into being, and going out of being. Apart from these there is the element of the Eternal Cosmos, which is "in accordance with nature," having its own natural and eternal motion ever the same. This is the fifth or divine element, the aetherial, by the schoolmen translated *Quinta Essentia*, whence by a curious degradation we have our modern word Quintessence, of that which is the finest and subtlest extract.

Still more clearly is the organic conception carried out in Aristotle's discussion of the Vital principle or Soul in the various grades of living creatures and in man. It will be sufficient to quote at length a chapter of Aristotle's treatise on the subject (*De Anima*, ii. p. 1) in which this fundamental conception of Aristotle's philosophy is very completely illustrated:—

"Now as to Substance we remark that this is one particular category among existences, having three different aspects. First there is, so to say, the raw material or Matter, having in it no definite character or quality; next the Form or Specific character, in virtue of which the thing becomes namable; and third, there is the Thing or Substance which these two together constitute. The Matter is, in other words, the *potentiality* of the thing, the Form is the *realization* of that potentiality.

We may further have this realization in two ways, corresponding in character to the distinction between *knowledge* (which we have but are not necessarily using) and actual *contemplation* or mental perception.

"Among substances as above defined those are most truly such which we call *bodily objects*, and among these most especially objects which are the products of nature, inasmuch as all other bodies must be derived from them. Now among such natural objects some are possessed of life, some are not; by *life* I mean a process of spontaneous nourishment, growth, and decay. Every natural object having life is a substance compounded, so to say, of several qualities. It is, in fact, a bodily substance defined in virtue of its having life. Between the living body thus defined and the Soul or Vital principle, a marked distinction must be drawn. The body cannot be said to 'subsist in' something else; rather must we say that it is the matter or substratum in which something else subsists. And what we mean by the soul is just this substance in the sense of the *form* or specific character that subsists in the natural body which is *potentially* living. In other words, the Soul is substance as *realization*, only, however, of such a body as has just been defined. Recalling now the distinction between realization as possessed knowledge and as actual contemplation, we shall see that in its essential nature the Soul or Vital principle corresponds rather with the first than with the second. For both sleep and waking depend on the Soul or Life being there, but of these waking only can be said to correspond with the active form of knowledge; sleep is rather to be compared with the state of having without being immediately conscious that we have. Now if we compare these two states in respect of their priority of development in a particular person, we shall see that the state of latent possession comes first. We may therefore define the Soul or Vital principle as *The earliest realization (entelechy) of a natural body having in it the potentiality of life*.

"To every form of organic structure this definition applies, for even the parts of plants are organs, although very simple ones; thus the outer leaf is a protection to the pericarp, and the pericarp to the fruit. Or, again, the roots are organs bearing an analogy to the mouth in animals, both serving to take in food. Putting our definition, then, into a form applicable to every stage of the Vital principle, we shall say that *The Soul is the earliest realization of a natural body having organization*.

"In this way we are relieved from the necessity of asking whether Soul and body are one. We might as well ask whether the wax and the impression are one, or, in short, whether the *matter* of any object and that whereof it is the matter or substratum are one. As has been pointed out, unity and substantiality may have several significations, but the truest sense of both is found in *realization*.

"The general definition of the Soul or Vital principle above given may be further explained as follows. The Soul is the *rational* substance (or function), that is to say, it is that which gives essential meaning and reality to a body as knowable. Thus if an axe were a *natural* instrument or organ, its rational substance would be found in its realization of what an axe means; this would be its *soul*. Apart from such realization it would not be an axe at all, except in name. Being, however, such as it is, the axe remains an axe independently of any such realization. For the statement that the Soul is the *reason* of a thing, that which gives it essential meaning and reality, does not apply to such objects as an axe, but only to natural bodies having power of spontaneous motion (including growth) and rest.

"Or we may illustrate what has been said by reference to the bodily members. If the eye be a living creature, *sight* will be its soul, for this is the *rational* substance (or function) of the eye. On the other hand, the eye itself is the *material* substance in which this function subsists, which function being gone, the eye would no longer be an eye, except in name, just as we can speak of the eye of a statue or of a painted form. Now apply this illustration from a part of the body to the whole. For as any one sense stands related to its organ, so does the vital sense in general to the whole sensitive organism as such, always remembering that we do not mean a dead body, but one which really has in it potential life, as the seed or fruit has. Of course there is a form of realization to which the name applies in a specially full sense, as when the axe is actually cutting, the eye actually seeing, the man fully awake. But the Soul or Vital principle corresponds rather with the *function* of sight, or the *capacity* for cutting which the axe has, the body, on the other hand, standing in a relation of *potentiality* to it. Now just as the eye may mean both the actual organ or pupil, and also the function of sight, so also the living creature means both the body and the soul. We cannot, therefore, think of body apart from soul, or soul apart from body. If, however, we regard the soul as composed of parts, we can see that the realization to which we give the name of soul is in some cases essentially a realization of certain parts of the body. We may, however, conceive the soul as in other aspects separable, in so far as the realization cannot be connected with any bodily parts. Nay, we cannot be certain whether the soul may not be the realization or perfection of the body as the sailor is of his boat."

Observe that at the last Aristotle, though very tentatively, leaves an opening for immortality, where, as in the case of man, there are functions of the soul, such as philosophic contemplation, which cannot be related to bodily conditions. He really was convinced that in man there was a portion of that diviner aether which dwelt eternally in the heavens, and was the ever-moving cause of all things. If there was in man a *passive* mind, which became all things, as all things through sensation affected it, there was also, Aristotle argued, a *creative* mind in man, which is above, and unmixed with, that which it apprehends, gives laws to this, is essentially prior to all particular knowledge, is therefore eternal, not subject to the conditions of time and space, consequently indestructible.

Finally, as a note on Aristotle's method, one may observe in this passage, *first*, Aristotle's use of 'defining examples,' the wax, the leaf and fruit, the axe, the eye, etc.; *second*, his practice of developing his distinctions gradually, Form and Matter in the abstract, then in substances of every kind, then in natural bodies, then in organic bodies of various grades, in separate organs, in the body as a whole, and in the Soul as separable in man; and *thirdly*, his method of approaching completeness in thought, by apparent contradictions or qualifications, which aim at meeting the complexity of nature by an equally organized complexity of analysis. To this let us simply add, by way of final characterization, that in the preceding pages we have given but the merest fragment here and there of Aristotle's vast accomplishment. So wide is the range of his ken, so minute his observation, so subtle and complicated and allusive his illustrations, that it is doubtful if any student of his, through all the centuries in which he has influenced the world, ever found life long enough to fairly and fully grasp him. Meanwhile he retains his grasp upon us. Form and matter, final and efficient causes, potential and actual existences, substance, accident, difference, genus, species, predication, syllogism, deduction, induction, analogy, and multitudes of other joints in the machinery of thought for all time, were forged for us in the workshop of Aristotle.

CHAPTER XXI

THE SCEPTICS AND EPICUREANS

Greek decay—The praises of Lucretius—Canonics—Physics—The proofs of Lucretius—The atomic soul—Mental pleasures—Natural pleasures—Lower philosophy and higher

Philosophy, equally complete, equally perfect in all its parts, had its final word in Plato and Aristotle; on the great lines of universal knowledge no further really original structures were destined to be raised by Greek hands. We have seen a parallelism between Greek philosophy and Greek politics in their earlier phases; the same parallelism continues to the end. Greece broke the bonds of her intense but narrow civic life and civic thought, and spread herself out over the world in a universal monarchy and a cosmopolitan philosophy; but with this widening of the area of her influence reaction came and disruption and decay; an immense stimulus was given on the one hand to the political activity, on the other, to the thought and knowledge of the world as a whole, but at the centre Greece was 'living Greece no more,' her politics sank to the level of a dreary farce, her philosophy died down to a dull and spiritless skepticism, to an Epicureanism that 'seasoned the wine-cup with the dust of death,' or to a Stoicism not undignified yet still sad and narrow and stern. The hope of the world, alike in politics and in philosophy, faded as the life of Greece decayed.

The first phase of the change, *Scepticism*, or Pyrrhonism, as it was named from its first teacher, need not detain us long. Pyrrho was priest of Elis; in earlier life he accompanied Alexander the Great as far as India, and is said to have become acquainted with certain of the philosophic sects in that country. In his skeptical doctrine he had, like his predecessors, a school with its succession of teachers; but the world has remembered little more of him or them than two phrases 'suspense of judgment'—this for the intellectual side of philosophy; 'impassibility'—this for the moral. The doctrine is a negation of doctrine, the idle dream of idle men; even Pyrrho once, when surprised in some sudden access of fear, confessed that it was hard for him 'to get rid of the man in himself.' Vigorous men and growing nations are never agnostic. They decline to rest in mere suspense; they are extremely the opposite of impassive; they believe earnestly, they feel strongly.

A more interesting, because more positive and constructive, personality was that of Epicurus. This philosopher was born at Samos, in the year 341 B.C., of Athenian parents. He came to Athens in his eighteenth year. Xenocrates was then teaching at the Academy, Aristotle at the Lyceum, but Epicurus heard neither the one nor the other. After some wanderings he returned to Athens and set up on his own account as a teacher of philosophy. He made it a matter of boasting that he was a self-taught philosopher; and Cicero (*De Nat. Deor.* i. 26) sarcastically remarks that one could have guessed as much, even if Epicurus had not stated it himself; as one might of the proprietor of an ugly house, who should boast that he had employed no architect. The style of Epicurus was, in fact, plain and unadorned, but he seems all the same to have been able to say what he meant; and few if any writers ancient or modern have ever had so splendid a literary tribute, as Epicurus had from the great Roman poet Lucretius, his follower and expositor.

"Glory of the Greek race," he says, "who first hadst power to raise high so bright a light in the midst of darkness so profound, shedding a beam on all the interests of life, thee do I follow, and in the markings of thy track do I set my footsteps now. Not that I desire to rival thee, but rather for love of thee would fain call myself thy disciple. For how shall the swallow rival the swan, or what speed may the kid with its tottering limbs attain, compared with the brave might of the scampering steed? Thou; O father, art the discoverer of nature, thou suppliest to us a father's teachings, and from thy pages, illustrious one, even as bees sip all manner of sweets along the flowery glades, we in like manner devour all thy golden words, golden and right worthy to live forever. For soon as thy philosophy, birth of thy godlike mind, hath begun to declare the origin of things, straightway the terrors of the soul are scattered, earth's walls are broken apart, and through all the void I see nature in the working. I behold the gods in manifestation of their power, I discern their blissful seats, which never winds assail nor rain-clouds sprinkle with their showers, nor snow falling white with hoary frost doth buffet, but cloudless aether ever wraps them round, beaming in broad diffusion of glorious light. For nature supplies their every want nor aught impairs their peace of soul. But nowhere do I see any regions of hellish darkness, nor does the earth impose a barrier to our sight of what is done in the void beneath our feet. Wherefore a holy ecstasy and thrill of awe possess me, while thus by thy power the secrets of nature are disclosed to view" (Lucret. *De Nat. Rer.* iii, 1-30).

This devotion to the memory of Epicurus on the part of Lucretius was paralleled by the love felt for him by his contemporaries; he had crowds of followers who loved him and who were proud to learn his words by heart. He seems indeed to have been a man of exceptional kindness and amiability, and the 'garden of Epicurus' became proverbial as a place of temperate pleasures and wise delights. Personally we may take it that Epicurus was a man of simple tastes and moderate desires; and indeed throughout its history Epicureanism as a rule of conduct has generally been associated with the finer forms of enjoyment, rather than the more sensual. The 'sensual sty' is a nickname, not a description.

Philosophy Epicurus defined as a process of thought and reasoning tending to the realization of happiness. Arts or sciences which had no such practical end he contemned; and, as will be observed in Lucretius' praises of him above, even physics had but one purpose or interest, to free the soul from terrors of the unseen. Thus philosophy was mainly concerned with conduct, *i.e.* with Ethics, but secondarily and negatively with Physics, to which was appended what Epicurus called Canonics, or the science of testing, that is, a kind of logic.

Beginning with *Canonics*, as the first part of philosophy in order of time, from the point of view of human knowledge, Epicurus laid it down that the only source of knowledge was the senses, which gave us an immediate and true perception of that which actually came into contact with them. Even the visions of madmen or of dreamers he considered were in themselves true, being produced by a physical cause of some kind, of which these visions were the direct and immediate report. Falsity came in with people's interpretations or imaginations with respect to these sensations.

Sensations leave a trace in the memory, and out of similarities or analogies among sensations there are developed in the mind general notions or types, such as 'man,' 'house,' which are also true, because they are reproductions of sensations. Thirdly, when a sensation occurs, it is brought into relation in the mind with one or more of these types or notions; this is *predication*, true also in so far as its elements are true, but capable of falsehood, as subsequent or independent sensation may prove. If supported or not contradicted by sensation, it is or may be true; if contradicted or not supported by sensation, it is or may be false. The importance of this statement of the canon of truth or falsehood will be understood when we come to the physics of Epicurus, at the basis of which is his theory of Atoms, which by their very nature can never be directly testified to by sensation.

This and no more was what Epicurus had to teach on the subject of logic. He had no theory of definition, or division, or ratiocination, or refutation, or explication; on all these matters Epicurus was, as Cicero said, 'naked and unarmed.' Like most self-taught or ill-taught teachers, Epicurus trusted to his dogmas; he knew nothing and cared nothing for logical defense.

In his *Physics* Epicurus did little more than reproduce the doctrine of Democritus. He starts from the fundamental proposition that 'nothing can be produced from nothing, nothing can really perish.' The veritable existences in nature are the Atoms, which are too minute to be discernible by the senses, but which nevertheless have a definite size, and cannot further be divided. They have also a definite weight and form, but no qualities other than these. There is an infinity of empty space; this Epicurus proves on abstract grounds, practically because a limit to space is unthinkable. It follows that there must be an infinite number of the atoms, otherwise they would disperse throughout the infinite void and disappear. There is a limit, however, to the number of varieties among the atoms in respect of form, size, and weight. The existence of the void space is proved by the fact that motion takes place, to which he adds the argument that it necessarily exists also to separate the atoms one from another. So far Epicurus and Democritus are agreed.

To the Democritean doctrine, however, Epicurus made a curious addition, to which he himself is said to have attached much importance. The natural course (he said) for all bodies having weight is downwards in a straight line. It struck Epicurus that this being so, the atoms would all travel for ever in parallel lines, and those 'clashings and interminglings' of atoms out of which he conceived all visible forms to be produced, could never occur. He therefore laid it down that the atoms *deviated* the least little bit from the straight, thus making a world possible. And Epicurus considered that this supposed deviation of the atoms not only made a world possible, but human freedom also. In the deviation, without apparent cause, of the descending atoms, the law of necessity was broken, and there was room on the one hand for man's free will, on the other, for prayer to the gods, and for hope of their interference on our behalf.

It may be worthwhile summarizing the proofs which Lucretius in his great poem, professedly following in the footsteps of Epicurus, adduces for these various doctrines.

Epicurus' first dogma is, 'Nothing proceeds from nothing,' that is, every material object has some matter previously existing exactly equal in quantity to it, out of which it was made. To prove this Lucretius appeals to the *order of nature* as seen in the seasons, in the phenomena of growth, in the fixed relations which exist between life and its environment as regards what is helpful or harmful, in the limitation of size and of faculties in the several species and the fixity of the characteristics generally in each, in the possibilities of cultivation and improvement of species within certain limits and under certain conditions.

To prove his second position, 'Nothing passes into nothing,' Lucretius points out to begin with that there is a law even in destruction; *force* is required to dissolve or dismember anything; were it otherwise the world would have disappeared long ago. Moreover, he points out that it is from the elements set free by decay and death that new things are built up; there is no waste, no visible lessening of the resources of nature, whether in the generations of living things, in the flow of streams and the fullness of ocean, or in the eternal stars. Were it not so, infinite time past would have exhausted all the matter in the universe, but Nature is clearly immortal. Moreover, there is a correspondence between the structure of bodies and the forces necessary to their destruction. Finally, apparent violations of the law, when carefully examined, only tend to confirm it. The rains no doubt disappear, but it is that their particles may reappear in the juices of the crops and the trees and the beasts which feed on them.

Nor need we be surprised at the doctrine that the atoms, so all-powerful in the formation of things, are themselves invisible. The same is true of the forest-rending blasts, the 'viewless winds' which lash the waves and overwhelm great fleets. There are odors also that float unseen upon the air; there are heat, and cold, and voices. There is the process of evaporation, whereby we know that the water has gone, yet cannot see its vapor departing. There is the gradual invisible detrition of rings upon the finger, of stones hollowed out by dripping water, of the ploughshare in the field, and the flags upon the streets, and the brazen statues of the gods whose fingers men kiss as they pass the gates, and the rocks that the salt sea-brine eats into along the shore.

That there is Empty Space or Void he proves by all the varied motions on land and sea which we behold; by the porosity even of hardest things, as we see in dripping caves. There is the food also which disperses itself throughout the body, in trees and cattle. Voices pass through closed doors, frost can pierce even to the bones. Things equal in size vary in weight; a lump of wool has more of void in it than a lump of lead. So much for Lucretius.

For abstract theories on physics, except as an adjunct and support to his moral conceptions, Epicurus seems to have had very little inclination. He thus speaks of the visible universe or Cosmos. The Cosmos is a sort of skyey enclosure, which holds within it the stars, the earth, and all visible things. It is cut off from the infinite by a wall of division which may be either rare or dense, in motion or at rest, round or three-cornered or any other form. That there is such a wall of division is quite admissible, for no object of which we have observation is without its limit. Were this wall of division to break, everything contained within it would tumble out. We may conceive that there are an infinite number of such Cosmic systems, with inter-cosmic intervals throughout the infinity of space.

He is very disinclined to assume that similar phenomena, *e.g.* eclipses of the sun or moon, always have the same cause. The various accidental implications and interminglings of the atoms may produce the same effect in various ways. In fact Epicurus has the same impatience of theoretical physics as of theoretical philosophy. He is a 'practical man.'

He is getting nearer his object when he comes to the nature of the soul. The soul, like everything else, is composed of atoms, extremely delicate and fine. It very much resembles the breath, with a mixture of heat thrown in, sometimes coming nearer in nature to the first, sometimes to the second. Owing to the delicacy of its composition it is extremely subject to variation, as we see in its passions and liability to emotion, its phases of thought and the varied experiences without which we cannot live. It is, moreover, the chief cause of sensation being possible for us. Not that it could of itself have had sensation, without the enwrapping support of the rest of the structure. The rest of the structure, in fact, having prepared this chief cause, gets from it a share of what comes to it, but not a share of all which the soul has.

The soul being of material composition equally with the other portions of the bodily structure, dies of course with it, that is, its particles like the rest are dispersed, to form new bodies. There is nothing dreadful therefore about death, for there is nothing left to know or feel anything about it.

As regards the process of sensation, Epicurus, like Democritus, conceived bodies as having a power of emitting from their surface extremely delicate images of themselves. These are composed of very fine atoms, but, in spite of their tenuity, they are able to maintain for a considerable time their relative form and order, though liable after a time to distortion. They fly with great celerity through the void, and find their way through the windows of the senses to the soul, which by its delicacy of nature is in sympathy with them, and apprehends their form.

The gods are indestructible, being composed of the very finest and subtlest atoms, so as to have not a body, but *as it were* a body. Their life is one of perfect blessedness and peace. They are in number countless; but the conceptions of the vulgar are erroneous respecting them. They are not subject to the passions of humanity. Anger and joy are alike alien to their nature; for all such feelings imply a lack of strength. They dwell apart in the inter-cosmic spaces. As Cicero jestingly remarks: "Epicurus by way of a joke introduced his gods so pure that you could see through them, so delicate that the wind could blow through them, having their dwelling-place outside between two worlds, for fear of breakage."

Coming finally to Epicurus' theory of Ethics, we find a general resemblance to the doctrine of Democritus and Aristippus. The end of life is pleasure or the absence of pain. He differs, however, from the Cyrenaics in maintaining that not the pleasure of the moment is the end, but pleasure throughout the whole of life, and that therefore we ought in our conduct to have regard to the future. Further he denies that pleasure exists only in activity, it exists equally in rest and quiet; in short, he places more emphasis in his definition on the absence of pain or disturbance, than on the presence of positive pleasure. And thirdly, while the Cyrenaics maintained that bodily pleasures and pains were the keenest, Epicurus claimed these characteristics for the pleasures of the mind, which intensified the present feeling by anticipations of the future and recollections of the past. And thus the wise man might be happy, even on the rack. Better indeed was it to be unlucky and wise, than lucky and foolish. In a similar temper Epicurus on his death-bed wrote thus to a friend: "In the enjoyment of blessedness and peace, on this the last day of my life I write this letter to you. Strangury has supervened, and the extremist agony of internal pains, yet resisting these has been my joy of soul, as I recalled the thoughts which I have had in the past."

We must note, however, that while mental pleasures counted for much with the Epicureans, these mental pleasures consisted not in thought for thought's sake in any form; they had nothing to do with contemplation. They were essentially connected with bodily experiences; they were the memory of past, the anticipation of future, bodily pleasures. For it is to be remembered that thoughts were with Epicurus only converted sensations, and sensations were bodily processes. Thus every joy of the mind was conditioned by a bodily experience preceding it. Or as Metrodorus, Epicurus' disciple, defined the matter: "A man is happy when his body is in good case, and he has good hope that it will continue so." Directly or indirectly, therefore, every happiness came back, in the rough phrase of Epicurus, to one's belly at last.

This theory did not, however, reduce morality to bestial self-indulgence. If profligate pleasures could be had free from mental apprehensions of another world and of death and pain and disease in this, and if they brought with them guidance as to their own proper restriction, there would be no reason whatever to blame a man for filling himself to the full of pleasures, which brought no pain or sorrow, that is, no evil, in their train. But (Epicurus argues) this is far from being the case. Moreover there are many pleasures keen enough at the time, which are by no means pleasant in the remembering. And even when we have them they bring no enjoyment to the highest parts of our nature. What those 'highest parts' are, and by what standard their relative importance is determined, Epicurus does not say. He probably meant those parts of our nature which had the widest range in space and time, our faculties, namely, of memory and hope, of conception, of sight and hearing.

Moreover there are distinctions among desires; some are both natural and compulsory, such as thirst; some are natural but not compulsory, as the desire for dainties; some are neither natural nor compulsory, such as the desire for crowns or statues. The last of these the wise man will contemn, the second he will admit, but so as to retain his freedom. For independence of such things is desirable, not necessarily that we may reduce our wants to a minimum, but in order that if we cannot enjoy many things, we may be content with few. "For I am convinced," Epicurus continues, "that they have the greatest enjoyment of wealth, who are least dependent upon it for enjoyment."

Thus if Epicurus did not absolutely teach simplicity of living, he taught his disciples the necessity of being capable of such simplicity, which they could hardly be without practice. So that in reality the doctrine of Epicurus came very near that of his opponents. As Seneca the Stoic observed, "Pleasure with him comes to be something very thin and pale. In fact that law which we declare for virtue, the same law he lays down for pleasure."

One of the chief and highest pleasures of life Epicurus found in the possession of friends, who provided for each other not only help and protection, but a lifelong joy. For the 'larger friendship' of the civic community, Epicurus seems to have had only a very neutral regard. Justice, he says, is a convention of interests, with a view of neither hurting or being hurt. The wise man will have nothing to do with politics, if he can help it.

In spite of much that may offend in the doctrines of Epicurus, there is much at least in the man which is sympathetic and attractive. What one observes, however, when we compare such a philosophy with that of Plato or Aristotle, is first, a total loss of constructive imagination. The parts of the 'philosophy,' if we are so to call it, of Epicurus hang badly together, and neither the Canonics nor the Physics show any real faculty of serious thinking at all. The Ethics has a wider scope and a more real relation to experience if not to reason. But it can never satisfy the deeper apprehension of mankind.

The truest and most permanently valid revelations of life come not to the many but to the one or the few, who communicate the truth to the many, sometimes at the cost of their own lives, always at the cost of antagonism and ridicule. A philosophy therefore which only represents in theoretical form the average practice of the average man, comes into the world still-born. It has nothing to say; its hearers know it all, and the exact value of it all, already. And in their heart of hearts, many even of those who have stooped to a lower ideal, and sold their birthright of hopes beyond the passing hour, for a mess of pottage in the form of material success and easy enjoyment, have a lurking contempt for the preachers of what they practice; as many a slaveholder in America probably had for the clerical defenders of the 'divine institution.'

There is a wasting sense of inadequacy in this 'hand-to-mouth' theory of living, which compels most of those who follow it to tread softly and speak moderately. They are generally a little weary if not cynical; they don't think much of themselves or of their success; but they prefer to hold on as they have begun, rather than launch out into new courses, which they feel they have not the moral force to continue. "May I die," said the Cynic, "rather than lead a life of pleasure." "May I die," says the Epicurean, "rather than make a fool of myself." The Idealist is to them, if not a hypocrite, at least a visionary,—if not a Tartuffe, at least a Don Quixote tilting at windmills. Yet even for poor Don Quixote, with all his blindness and his follies, the world retains a sneaking admiration. It can spare a few or a good many of its worldly-wisdoms, rather than lose altogether its enthusiasms and its dreams. And the one thing which saves Epicureanism from utter extinction as a theory, is invariably the idealism which like a 'purple patch' adorns it here and there. No man and no theory is wholly self-centered. Pleasure is supplanted by Utility, and Utility becomes the greatest Happiness of the greatest Number, and so, as Horace says (*Ep.* I. x. 24)—

Naturam expellas furca, tamen usque recurret,

Nature (like Love) thrust out of the door, will come back by the window; and the Idealism which is not allowed to make pain a pleasure, is required at last to translate pleasure into pains.

CHAPTER XXII

THE STOICS

Semitic admixture—Closed fist and open hand—'Tabula rasa'—Necessity of evil—
Hymn of Cleanthes—Things indifferent—Ideal and real—Philosophy and humanity

Zeno, the founder of the Stoic school of philosophy (born *circa* 340 B.C.), was a native of Citium in Cyprus. The city was Greek, but with a large Phoenician admixture. And it is curious that in this last and sternest phase of Greek thought, not the founder only, but a large proportion of the successive leaders of the school, came from this and other places having Semitic elements in them. Among these places notable as nurseries of Stoicism was Tarsus in Cilicia, the birthplace of St. Paul. The times of preparation were drawing to a close; and through these men, with their Eastern intensity and capacities of self-searching and self-abasement, the philosophy of Greece was linking itself on to the wisdom of the Hebrews.

Zeno came to Athens to study philosophy, and for twenty years he was a pupil first of Crates the Cynic, and then of other teachers. At length he set up a school of his own in the celebrated *Stoa Poecile* (Painted Colonnade), so named because it was adorned with frescoes by Polygnotus. There he taught for nearly sixty years, and voluntarily ended his life when close on a century old. His life, as Antigonus, King of Macedon, recorded on his tomb, was consistent with his doctrine— abstemious, frugal, laborious, dutiful. He was succeeded by Cleanthes, a native of Assos in Asia Minor. But the great constructor of the Stoic doctrine, without whom, as his contemporaries said, there had been no Stoic school at all, was Chrysippus, a native of Soli or of Tarsus in Cilicia. He wrote at enormous length, supporting his teachings by an immense erudition, and culling liberally from the poets to illustrate and enforce his views. Learned and pedantic, his works had no inherent attraction, and nothing of them but fragments has been preserved. We know the Stoic doctrine mainly from the testimony and criticisms of later times.

Like the Epicureans, Zeno and his successors made philosophy primarily a search for the chief good, a doctrine of practice and morals. But like them they were impelled to admit a logic and a physics, at least by way of preliminary basis to their ethics. The relations of the three they illustrated by various images. Philosophy was like an animal; logic was its bones and sinews, ethics its flesh, physics its life or soul. Or again, philosophy was an egg; logic was the shell, ethics the white, physics, the yolk. Or again, it was a fruitful field; logic was the hedge, ethics the crop, physics the soil. Or it was a city, well ordered and strongly fortified, and so on. The images seem somewhat confused, but the general idea is clear enough. Morality was the essential, the living body, of philosophy; physics supplied its raw material, or the conditions under which a moral life could be lived; logic secured that we should use that material rightly and wisely for the end desired.

Logic the Stoics divided into two parts—Rhetoric, the 'science of the open hand,' and Dialectic, the 'science of the closed fist,' as Zeno called them. They indulged in elaborate divisions and subdivisions of each, with which we need not meddle. The only points of interest to us are contained in their analysis of the processes of perception and thought. A sensation, Zeno taught, was the result of an external *impulse*, which when combined with an internal *assent*, produced a mental state that revealed at the same time itself and the external object producing it. The perception thus produced he compared to the grip which the hand took of a solid object; and real perceptions, those, that is, which were caused by a real external object, and not by some illusion, always testified to the reality of their cause by this sensation of 'grip.'

The internal assent of the mind was voluntary, and at the same time necessary; for the mind could not do otherwise than will the acceptance of that which it was fitted to receive. The peculiarity of their physics, which we shall have to refer to later on, namely, the denial of the existence of anything not material, implied that in some way there was a material action of the external object on the structure of the perceiving mind (itself also material). What exactly the nature of this action was the Stoics themselves were not quite agreed. The idea of an 'impression' such as a seal makes upon wax was a tempting one, but they had difficulty in comprehending how there could be a multitude of different impressions on the same spot without effacing each other. Some therefore preferred the vaguer and safer expression, 'modification'; had they possessed our modern science, they might have illustrated their meaning by reference to the phenomena of magnetism or electricity.

An interesting passage may be quoted from Plutarch on the Stoic doctrine of knowledge: "The Stoics maintain," he says, "that when a human being is born, he has the governing part of his soul like a sheet of paper ready prepared for the reception of writing, and on this the soul inscribes in succession its various ideas. The first form of the writing is produced through the senses. When we perceive, for example, a white object, the recollection remains when the object is gone. And when many similar recollections have accumulated, we have what is called *experience*. Besides the ideas which we get in this natural and quite undersigned way, there are other ideas which we get through teaching and information. In the strict sense only these latter ought to be called ideas; the former should rather be called perceptions. Now the rational faculty, in virtue of which we are called reasoning beings, is developed out of, or over and beyond, the mass of perceptions, in the second seven years' period of life. In fact a thought may be defined as a kind of mental image, such as a rational animal alone is capable of having."

Thus there are various gradations of mental apprehensions; first, those of sensible qualities obtained through the action of the objects and the assent of the perceiving subject, as already described; then by experience, by comparison, by analogy, by the combinations of the reasoning faculty, further and more general notions are arrived at, and conclusions formed, as, for example, that the gods exist and exercise a providential care over the world. By this faculty also the wise man ascends to the apprehension of the good and true.

The physics of the Stoics started from the fundamental proposition that in the universe of things there were two elements—the active and the passive. The latter was Matter or unqualified existence; the former was the reason or qualifying element in Matter, that is, God, who being eternal, is the fashioner of every individual thing throughout the universe of matter. God is One; He is Reason, and Fate, and Zeus. In fact all the gods are only various representations of His faculties and powers. He being from the beginning of things by Himself, turneth all existence through air to water. And even as the genital seed is enclosed in the semen, so also was the seed of the world concealed in the water, making its matter apt for the further birth of things; then first it brought into being the four elements—fire, water, air, earth. For there was a finer fire or air which was the moving spirit of things; later and lower than this were the material elements of fire and air. It follows that the universe of things is threefold; there is first God Himself, the source of all character and individuality, who is indestructible and eternal, the fashioner of all things, who in certain cycles of ages gathers up all things into Himself, and then out of Himself brings them again to birth; there is the matter of the universe whereon God works; and thirdly, there is the union of the two. Thus the world is governed by reason and forethought, and this reason extends through every part, even as the soul or life extends to every part of us. The universe therefore is a living thing, having a soul or reason in it. This soul or reason one teacher likened to the air, another to the sky, another to the sun. For the soul of nature is, as it were, a finer air or fire, having a power of creation in it, and moving in an ordered way to the production of things.

The universe is one and of limited extension, being spherical in form, for this is the form which best adapts itself to movement. Outside this universe is infinite bodiless space; but within the universe there is no empty part; all is continuous and united, as is proved by the harmony of relation which exists between the heavenly bodies and those upon the earth. The world as such is destructible, for its parts are subject to change and to decay; yet is this change or destruction only in respect of the qualities imposed upon it from time to time by the Reason inherent in it; the mere unqualified Matter remains indestructible.

In the universe evil of necessity exists; for evil being the opposite of good, where no evil is there no good can be. For just as in a comedy there are absurdities, which are in themselves bad, but yet add a certain attraction to the poem as a whole, so also one may blame evil regarded in itself, yet for the whole it is not without its use. So also God is the cause of death equally with birth; for even as cities when the inhabitants have multiplied overmuch, remove their superfluous members by colonization or by war, so also is God a cause of destruction. In man in like manner good cannot exist save with evil; for wisdom being a knowledge of good and evil, remove the evil and wisdom itself goes. Disease and other natural evils, when looked at in the light of their effects, are means not of evil but of good; there is throughout the universe a balance and interrelation of good and evil. Not that God hath in Himself any evil; the law is not the cause of lawlessness, nor God Himself responsible for any violation of right.

The Stoics indulged in a strange fancy that the world reverted after a mighty cycle of years in all its parts to the same form and structure which it possessed at the beginning, so that there would be once more a Socrates, a Plato, and all the men that had lived, each with the same friends and fellow-citizens, the same experiences, and the same endeavors. At the termination of each cycle there was a burning up of all things, and thereafter a renewal of the great round of life.

Nothing incorporeal, they maintained, can be affected by or affect that which is corporeal; body alone can affect body. The soul therefore must be corporeal. Death is the separation of soul from body, but it is impossible to separate what is incorporeal from body; therefore, again, the soul must be corporeal. In the belief of Cleanthes, the souls of all creatures remained to the next period of cyclic conflagration; Chrysippus believed that only the souls of the wise and good remained.

Coming finally to the Ethics of the Stoic philosophy, we find for the chief end of life this definition, 'A life consistent with itself,' or, as it was otherwise expressed, 'A life consistent with Nature.' The two definitions are really identical; for the law of nature is the law of our nature, and the reason in our being the reason which also is in God, the supreme Ruler of the universe. This is substantially in accordance with the celebrated law of right action laid down by Kant, "Act so that the maxim of thine action be capable of being made a law of universal action." Whether a man act thus or no, by evil if not by good the eternal law will satisfy itself; the question is of import only for the man's own happiness. Let his will accord with the universal will, then the law will be fulfilled, and the man will be happy. Let his will resist the universal will, then the law will be fulfilled, but the man will bear the penalty. This was expressed by Cleanthes in a hymn which ran somewhat thus—

> Lead me, O Zeus most great,
> And thou, Eternal Fate:
> What way soe'er thy will doth bid me travel
> That way I'll follow without fret or cavil.

> Or if I evil be
> And spurn thy high decree,
> Even so I still shall follow, soon or late.

Thus in the will alone consists the difference of good or ill for us; in either case Nature's great law fulfils itself infallibly. To their view on this point we may apply the words of Hamlet: "If it be now, 'tis not to come; if it be not to come, it will be now; if it be not now, yet it will come; the *readiness* is all."

This universal law expresses itself in us in various successive manifestations. From the moment of birth it implants in us a supreme self-affection, whereby of infallible instinct we seek our own self-preservation, rejoice in that which is suitable to our existence, shrink from that which is unsuitable. As we grow older, further and higher principles manifest themselves—reason and reflection, a more and more careful and complete apprehension of that which is honourable and advantageous, a capacity of choice among goods. Till finally the surpassing glory of that which is just and honorable shines out so clear upon us, that any pain or loss is esteemed of no account, if only we may attain to that. Thus at last, by the very law of our being, we come to know that nothing is truly and absolutely good but goodness, nothing absolutely bad but sin. Other things, inasmuch as they have no character of moral good or moral evil, cannot be deemed really good or bad; in comparison with the absolutely good, they are things indifferent, though in comparison with each other they may be relatively preferable or relatively undesirable. Even pleasure and pain, so far as concerns the absolute end or happiness of our being, are things indifferent; we cannot call them either good or evil. Yet have they a relation to the higher law, for the consciousness of them was so implanted in us at the first that our souls by natural impulse are drawn to pleasure, while they shrink from pain as from a deadly enemy. Wherefore reason neither can nor ought to seek wholly to eradicate these primitive and deep-seated affections of our nature; but so to exercise a resisting and ordering influence upon them, as to render them obedient and subservient to herself.

That which is absolutely good—wisdom, righteousness, courage, temperance— does good only and never ill to us. All other things,—life, health, pleasure, beauty, strength, wealth, reputation, birth,—and their opposites,—death, disease, pain, deformity, weakness, poverty, contempt, humility of station,—these are in themselves neither a benefit nor a curse. They may do us good, they may do us harm. We may use them for good, we may use them for evil.

Thus the Stoics worked out on ideal and absolute lines the thought of righteousness as the chief and only good. Across this ideal picture were continually being drawn by opponents without or inquirers within, clouds of difficulty drawn from real experience. 'What,' it was asked, 'of *progress* in goodness? Is this a middle state between good and evil; or if a middle state between good and evil be a contradiction, in terms, how may we characterize it?' Here the wiser teachers had to be content to answer that it *tended* towards good, was good in possibility, would be absolutely good when the full attainment came, and the straining after right had been swallowed up in the perfect calm of settled virtue.

'How also of the wise man tormented by pain, or in hunger and poverty and rags, is his perfectness of wisdom and goodness really sufficient to make him happy?' Here, again, the answer had to be hesitating and provisional, through no fault of the Stoics. In this world, while we are still under the strange dominion of time and circumstance, the ideal can never wholly fit the real. There must still be difficulty and incompleteness here, only to be solved and perfected 'when iniquity shall have an end.' Our eyes may fail with looking upward, yet the upward look is well; and the jibes upon the Stoic 'king in rags' that Horace and others were so fond of, do not affect the question. It may have been, and probably often was, the case that Stoic teachers were apt to transfer to themselves personally the ideal attributes, which they justly assigned to the ideal man in whom wisdom was perfected. The doctrine gave much scope for cant and mental pride and hypocrisy, as every ideal doctrine does, including the Christian. But the existence of these vices in individuals no more affected the doctrine of an ideal goodness in its Stoic form, than it does now in its Christian one. That only the good man is truly wise or free or happy; that vice, however lavishly it surround itself with luxury and ease and power, is inherently wretched and foolish and slavish;—these are things which are worth saying and worth believing, things, indeed, which the world dare not and cannot permanently disbelieve, however difficult or even impossible it may be to mark men off into two classes, the good and the bad, however strange the irony of circumstance which so often shows the wicked who 'are not troubled as other men, neither are they plagued like other men; they have more than their heart could wish,' while good men battle with adversity, often in vain. Still will the permanent, fruitful, progressive faith of man 'look to the end'; still will the ideal be powerful to plead for the painful right, and spoil, even in the tasting, the pleasant wrong.

The doctrine, of course, like every doctrine worth anything, was pushed to extravagant lengths, and thrust into inappropriate quarters, by foolish doctrinaires. As that the wise man is the only orator, critic, poet, physician, nay, cobbler if you please; that the wise man knows all that is to be known, and can do everything that is worth doing, and so on. The school was often too academic, too abstract, too fond of hearing itself talk. This, alas! is what most schools are, and most schoolmasters.

Yet the Stoics were not altogether alien to the ordinary interests and duties of life. They admitted a duty of co-operating in politics, at least in such states as showed some desire for, or approach to, virtue. They approved of the wise man taking part in education, of his marrying and bringing up children, both for his own sake and his country's. He will be ready even to 'withdraw himself from life on behalf of his country or his friends. This 'withdrawal,' which was their word for suicide, came unhappily to be much in the mouths of later, and especially of the Roman, Stoics, who, in the sadness and restraint of prevailing despotism, came to thank God that no one was compelled to remain in life; he might 'withdraw' when the burden of life, the hopelessness of useful activity, became too great.

With this sad, stern, yet not undignified note, the philosophy of Greece speaks its last word. The later skepticism of the New Academy, directed mainly to a negative criticism of the crude enough logic of the Stoics, or of the extravagances of their ethical doctrine, contributed no substantial element to thought or morals. As an eclectic system it had much vogue, side by side with Stoicism and Epicureanism, among the Romans, having as its chief exponent Cicero, as Epicureanism had Lucretius, and Stoicism, Seneca.

The common characteristic of all these systems in their later developments, is their *cosmopolitanism. Homo sum, nil humani a me alienum puto,* 'I am a man; nothing appertaining to humanity do I deem alien from myself,' this was the true keynote of whatever was vital in any of them. And the reason of this is not far to seek. We have seen already how the chaos of sophistic doctrine was largely conditioned, if not produced, by the breakdown of the old civic life of Greece. The process hardly suffered delay from all the efforts of Socrates and Plato. Cosmopolitanism was already a point of union between the Cynics and Cyrenaics . And the march of politics was always tending in the same direction. First through great leagues, such as the Spartan or Athenian or Theban, each with a predominant or tyrannical city at the head; then later through the conquest of Greece by Alexander, and the leaguing of all Greek-speaking peoples in the great invasion of Asia; then through the spread of Greek letters all over the Eastern world, and the influx upon Greek centers such as Athens and Alexandria, of all manner of foreign intelligences; and finally, through the conquest of all this teeming world of culture by the discipline and practical ability of Rome, and its incorporation in a universal empire of law, all the barriers which had divided city from city and tribe from tribe and race from race disappeared, and only a common humanity remained.

The only effective philosophies for such a community were those which regarded man as an *individual*, with a world politically omnipotent hedging him about, and driving him in upon himself. Thus the New Academy enlarged on the doubtfulness of all beyond the individual consciousness; Stoicism insisted on individual dutifulness, Epicureanism on individual self-satisfaction. The first sought to make life worth living through culture, the second through indifference, the third through a moderate enjoyment. But all alike felt themselves very helpless in face of the growing sadness of life, in face of the deepening mystery of the world beyond. All alike were controversial, and quick enough to ridicule their rivals; none was hopefully constructive, or (unless in the poetic enthusiasm of a Lucretius) very confident of the adequacy of its own conceptions. They all rather quickened the sense of emptiness in human existence, than satisfied it; at the best they enabled men to "absent themselves a little while from the felicity of death."

Thus all over the wide area of Greek and Roman civilization, the activity of the later schools was effectual to familiarize humanity with the language of philosophy, and to convince humanity of the inadequacy of its results. Both of these things the Greeks taught to Saul of Tarsus; at a higher Source he found the satisfying of his soul; but from the Greek philosophies he learned the language through which the new Revelation was to be taught in the great world of Roman rule and Grecian culture. And thus through the Pauline theology, Greek philosophy had its part in the moral regeneration of the world; as it has had, in later times, in every emancipation and renascence of its thought.

www.ingramcontent.com/pod-product-compliance
Lightning Source LLC
Chambersburg PA
CBHW060944040426
42445CB00011B/988